Young people in post-conflict Northern Ireland

The past cannot be changed, but the future can be developed

Edited by

Dirk Schubotz and Paula Devine

Russell House Publishing

First published in 2008 by:
Russell House Publishing Ltd
4 St. George's House
Uplyme Road
Lyme Regis
Dorset DT7 3LS

Tel: 01297-443948
Fax: 01297-442722

e-mail: help@russellhouse.co.uk
www.russellhouse.co.uk

British Library Cataloguing-in-publication Data:

A catalogue record for this book is available from the British Library.

ISBN: 978-1-905541-34-8

Typeset by TW Typesetting, Plymouth, Devon
Printed by Biddles, King's Lynn

About Russell House Publishing

Russell House Publishing aims to publish innovative and valuable materials to help managers, practitioners, trainers, educators and students.

Our full catalogue covers: social policy, working with young people, helping children and families, care of older people, social care, combating social exclusion, revitalising communities and working with offenders.

Full details can be found at www.russellhouse.co.uk and we are pleased to send out information to you by post. Our contact details are on this page.

We are always keen to receive feedback on publications and new ideas for future projects.

Contents

Preface

The Northern Ireland conflict has been one of the most thoroughly researched conflicts in the world. So, what has this book to offer beyond what has already been said about Northern Ireland?

We believe that the cessation of paramilitary violence opens up the opportunity to focus on issues affecting young people which in the past have been overlooked due to the sheer impact that the Northern Ireland conflict has had on the lives of people living here. A side effect of this conflict is also that relatively little has been communicated about the lives and times of young people growing up in Northern Ireland which goes beyond conflict-related information on violence, paramilitary activities, sectarianism and segregation. We have been systematically collecting attitudinal data since 1998 and now feel that we have gathered sufficient material to offer this to a wider audience in this volume.

This is a timely book as the first generation of young people from Northern Ireland is now coming of age with no personal memories of the 'Troubles'.

The book is thus an opportunity to reflect on the issues faced by young people in societies like Northern Ireland that come out of conflict or experience substantial societal change. From that point of view it is a critically important resource that will appeal to anyone working with young people or being interested in this unique and crucial time in Northern Ireland's history.

At the same time this book gives evidence that underneath the sectarian surface, young people have grown up with all the same issues, desires and opportunities as other young people elsewhere of today's 'txt generation'. Therefore the book also contains messages for people working with 16-year-olds in all other parts of the UK, of Ireland and beyond.

For all such readers, this multi-faceted study across different parts of young people's lives and communities can act as a powerful reminder that making a difference requires us to work across all parts of their lives, not just on those that present themselves immediately.

This book looks beyond what many expect to hear about when Northern Ireland is being discussed: violence, sectarianism, segregated schooling, cross-community conflict and tribal politics. It also discusses how parallel to the peace processes issues like inward migration, mental health, suicide rates, bullying and pupil participation, sexual health and poverty have gained momentum in the policy arena of a society coming out of conflict. What is more, this book also provides an insider perspective to this all through the publication of a prize-winning essay from a competition that was open to all Northern Ireland's 16-year olds in 2007.

In the final chapter we reflect on methodological challenges in providing an academically robust yet participatory research vehicle that allows us to continue to collect young people's views on issues that are relevant and important to them.

The Editors

Foreword

Articulating the diverse and poignant experiences of young people growing up in Northern Ireland at a time of rapid change and uncertainty, but also considerable hope for the future, this book captures a unique passage of time through the eyes of young citizens making transitions of their own.

It achieves this by drawing on survey data from the Young Life and Times* survey which records the attitudes of 16-year-olds living in Northern Ireland to a range of social issues:

- Has the ability to communicate the experiences of young people to a wider audience in a way that is even-handed, clear and accessible.
- Actively involved young people in identifying the issues surveyed, making YLT an unusually democratic and participatory resource.

The themes emerging in the following chapters – community relations, pupil voice, social disadvantage, sexual and mental health, bullying – are issues that will have a poignancy for young people from across the UK, Europe and beyond.

We hope that this book helps improve the understanding readers have of young lives in contemporary society and, at the same time, lead to a clearer consciousness in which young people are regarded not merely as a challenge for adult society, but as vibrant, creative and productive citizens willing and able to improve the communities in which they live.

In Northern Ireland there is the potential for young citizens to achieve a unique settlement with adult decision-makers, where their experiences and concerns are clearly understood and valued. This book, and the survey which informs it, will help this process considerably.

Carnegie UK Trust, ARK, YLT and the young people of Northern Ireland

The strong commitment to youth voice at ARK, and the ethos that has seen them experiment with new forms of participatory research reflects the values the Carnegie UK Trust promotes.

---

*YLT is a constituent part of ARK, an initiative by the two universities in Northern Ireland, which aims to make social and political information on Northern Ireland available to the widest possible audience.

For ten years, until 2007, the Trust ran a programme which promoted the wider influence of young people over decisions made about their lives. During that time we funded over 100 projects across the UK and the Republic of Ireland which were either shaped by young people or in which young people had a key role. We also published research, advocated for change with policy makers, established practitioner networks and towards the end of the programme initiated with partner organisations the 'Participation Works' consortium (www.participationworks.org) to provide a repertoire of support to organisations seeking to improve their practice of youth engagement.

So, the Carnegie United Kingdom Trust was extremely pleased to be able to support the Young Life and Times (YLT) survey.

Robert Bell, Carnegie United Kingdom Trust

Introduction

Paula Devine and Dirk Schubotz

The Northern Ireland conflict is one of the most thoroughly researched conflicts in the world (Smyth and Darby, 2001). Whole libraries could be filled with publications concerned with the effects that the so-called 'Troubles' have had on people living in Northern Ireland and beyond. In 1993 a register of conflict-related research in Northern Ireland (Ó'Máolain, 1993) revealed that there were 605 projects undertaken on the subject, an enormous number considering the small size of Northern Ireland, and there has not really been a noticeable decline in conflict-related research since the peace process began. Children and young people have been the focus of many of these projects, since they were particularly vulnerable to the paramilitary and sectarian violence in the three decades of conflict in Northern Ireland. Research about the human impact of the 'Troubles' on Northern Irish communities found that those under the age of 24 accounted for 40 per cent of conflict-related deaths (Faye, Morrissey and Smyth, 1999). Socio-religious segregation intensified from the late 1960s onwards, and the effects of segregated education and residency on community cohesion has also been widely researched from different angles: politically, psychologically and sociologically, to name but three. So, what has this book to offer beyond what has already been said about Northern Ireland?

Since the mid 1990s Northern Ireland has experienced significant societal change. The main paramilitary organisations have declared that 'the war is over' and ceased their activities. Albeit still very vulnerable, the Northern Ireland peace process has progressed beyond what would have been expected in the 1990s. The fact that the two parties (DUP and Sinn Féin) which have held the staunchest and most opposing views in relation to the way the Northern Ireland conflict should be resolved are now sharing power in a devolved Northern Ireland Assembly and Executive could be seen as evidence that there is now a shared commitment to creating a peaceful Northern Ireland regardless of its constitutional future.

We believe that the cessation of paramilitary violence opens up the opportunity to focus on issues affecting young people which in the past have been overlooked due to the sheer impact that the Northern Ireland conflict has had on the lives of people living here. In this way, this book is not merely a book about Northern Ireland, but it provides an opportunity to reflect on the issues faced by young people in societies that come out of conflict or experience substantial societal change.

About the surveys behind this book

All contributions in this book are based on data collected by the Young Life and Times (YLT) survey, which is undertaken by ARK on an annual basis. ARK is a joint initiative by academics from the two Northern Ireland universities – Queen's University Belfast and the University of Ulster. The YLT surveys have collected the views, attitudes and experiences of young people living in Northern Ireland on a range of social issues since 1998. From 1998 to 2000, a YLT survey ran alongside its sister survey, the Northern Ireland Life and Times (NILT) survey. This latter project records the attitudes and values of adults aged 18 years and over in Northern Ireland. However, in 2001, the survey team undertook a review of YLT since the level of use of the young person's survey came nowhere near the level of use of the adult survey. Based on these findings, an amended methodology was introduced in 2003. YLT is now an annual survey giving a representative sample of approximately 2,000 16-year olds living in Northern Ireland the chance to tell us about their lives. A core set of questions are included each year, for example, experiences of school and health, and views on politics and sectarianism. A range of other questions are asked less frequently. Significantly, each year YLT also includes a number of questions proposed by the previous year's respondents. (More details about the survey can be found in Appendix 1 of this book.)

The YLT survey is quite unique as it is a reliable, robust annual and ongoing project which allows us to monitor changes in attitudes and behaviour over time.

Children and young people in Northern Ireland

The interest in young people's issues in Northern Ireland at the present time is tremendous. For example, there is a dedicated Children and Young People's Unit at the Office of the First Minister and Deputy First Minister. As well as that, the post of Northern Ireland Commissioner for Children and Young People was established in 2003. The Commissioner's Office has been working on a multitude of issues concerning children's and young people's rights and

wellbeing. There are numerous statutory, charitable and voluntary organisations working in Northern Ireland that lobby and provide services for young
people. In addition, there is a substantial research community in all corners of
the globe whose interest is the changing Northern Irish society in particular.

About this book

We have invited some of the most well-known academics and social policy
makers in Northern Ireland to contribute to this book, to present their views
on the challenges which this first post-conflict generation faces in the new
Northern Ireland. These authors are nationally or internationally recognised
experts in their field. Whilst this book gives evidence that the effects of the
'Troubles' will continue to shape young people's lives for the foreseeable
future, in terms of school experiences, socio-economic conditions and mental
and sexual health, the contributions in this book also reveal some of the
pressures that many 16-year olds face regardless of where they live. Together
with the prize-winning essay of **Shaun Mulvenna** who offers his own insider
perspective as a 16-year old, the chapters in this book provide comprehensive
and compelling insight into key issues facing the 'txt generation'.

Most contributions in this book focus on the findings of the YLT surveys
conducted since 2003. Thus it is based on the attitudes and experiences of
young people living in Northern Ireland who can be regarded as the first
post-conflict generation as the first years of their lives coincided with the
beginning of the Northern Ireland peace process. What most of them have in
common is that, unlike their parents and grandparents, they have no active
personal memory of the worst conflict-related atrocities, even though they are
likely to have come across some form of sectarianism.

Firstly, in his chapter, **Duncan Morrow** explores community relations in
Northern Ireland. In particular, he focuses on issues related to the Northern
Ireland conflict, such as cross-community contact, experiences of violence and
sectarianism and factors which influence attitudes to each other. The chapter
also highlights the new Northern Ireland, which has most recently experienced
substantial inward migration, in particular from Eastern Europe, Portugal and
South Asia.

In the second chapter, **Katrina Lloyd, Ed Cairns, Claire Doherty** and **Kate
Ellis** discuss mental health issues of young people in Northern Ireland. The

relationship between mental health and stress is explored within the context of school. The authors also investigate whether increasing suicide rates among young people in Northern Ireland are in any way reflected in an overall decline in mental health.

Within her chapter on tackling bullying in schools, **Ruth Sinclair** looks at lessons to be learned for pupil participation in general. The data for this chapter comes not only from the YLT survey, but from a qualitative follow-up project undertaken in both primary and post-primary schools. The chapter asks how pupil participation can be a means of reducing incidences of school bullying whilst relating the specific findings on school bullying policies to a more general perspective on how pupils' participation in schools can be enhanced.

Simon Blake's chapter on sexual health advocacy work for young people looks at YLT findings relating to experiences of sex education and sexual intercourse, as well as social pressures to engage in sexual activity, and addresses the challenges that arise from this. The author relates the findings from respective YLT surveys to his personal experiences of working for a leading UK provider of sexual health services for young people. The possibilities of sexual health advocacy work for young people are explored in this chapter.

The education system in Northern Ireland is at a time of flux, with the transfer procedure at age 11 years due to be phased out in Northern Ireland after 2008. Currently this is one of the most contentious policy issues in Northern Ireland and the outcomes of this discussion are closely monitored by educationalists who consider the reintroduction of transfer tests in Britain. Within the UK more generally, the role of faith schools is being increasingly debated, and again the *de facto* religiously segregated school system in Northern Ireland can provide some lessons on the impact of segregated education on educational outcome and social attitudes. Thus, it is timely that **Tony Gallagher**'s chapter looks at the school experiences of pupils in Northern Ireland.

Unemployment rates in Northern Ireland are now among the lowest in the UK. Lower rates only exist in the south west of Great Britain (DETINI, 2008). Despite an overall increasing national wealth, poverty continues within society today because wealth remains unevenly distributed. Within their chapter on young people and social disadvantage, **Alex Tennant** and **Marina Monteith** look at the economic conditions of 16-year olds today and how poverty and class impact on a number of experiences and attitudes. They relate YLT findings to other research undertaken by Save the Children on the persistent poverty of children and young people.

A key feature of the YLT research project is the participation of young people, not only in completing the questionnaire, but also in suggesting topics for the following year's survey. In 2007, YLT respondents as well as all 16-year old school pupils were also invited to take part in an essay-writing competition. All participants were asked to submit an essay on what they think encapsulates 'The Life and Times of 16-year olds in Northern Ireland today'. We were very pleased with the high standard of submissions to this competition, and delighted to include the winning essay 'Is Anybody Listening?' by **Shaun Mulvenna** in this book. By doing so, we continue our commitment to give young people themselves a voice in the debate about issues that concern them.

In the final chapter, we review the methodological challenges for the YLT project, especially given our aim of recording the views of 16-year olds in Northern Ireland. Equally important, how can we enable these voices to have an impact on research and policy making relating to young people in Northern Ireland and beyond?

References

DETINI (Department of Trade and Investment in Northern Ireland) (2008): *Monthly Labour Market Report. January 2008*. Belfast: DETINI. Statistics Research Branch. Available online at: www.detini.gov.uk/cgi-bin/down-doc?id=3417 [Accessed 31 January 2008]

Faye, M., Morrisey, M. and Smyth, M. (1999) *Northern Ireland's Troubles: The Human Costs*. London: Pluto Press.

Ó Máolain, Ciarán (Ed.) (1993) *Register of Research on Northern Ireland. 1993 Edition*. Coleraine: University of Ulster.

Smyth, M. and Darby, J. (2001) Does Research Make Any Difference? The Case of Northern Ireland. In Smyth, M. and Robinson, G. (Eds.) *Researching Violently Divided Societies*. London: Pluto Press.

About the Authors

The Editors

Dirk Schubotz is Young Life and Times Director of ARK and is based at the School of Sociology, Social Policy and Social Work at Queen's University Belfast.

Paula Devine is Research Director of ARK and is based at the School of Sociology, Social Policy and Social Work at Queen's University Belfast.

The Contributors

Robert Bell was Director of the Carnegie Young People Initiative (CYPI) from 2003 until it ended in 2007. CYPI was a programme of the Carnegie United Kingdom Trust, which supported the Young Life and Times survey financially. Robert is now Social Justice Programme Manager at the Paul Hamlyn Foundation in London.

Simon Blake is Chief Executive Officer of Brook, the UK's national voluntary sector provider of free and confidential sexual health advice and services for young people under 25.

Ed Cairns is Professor of Psychology at the University of Ulster in Coleraine.

Claire Doherty is a student of Psychology at the University of Ulster in Coleraine.

Kate Ellis is a student of Psychology at the University of Ulster in Coleraine.

Tony Gallagher is Head of the School of Education at Queen's University Belfast.

Katrina Lloyd is Research Director of ARK and is based at the School of Sociology, Social Policy and Social Work at Queen's University Belfast.

Marina Monteith is Child Poverty Researcher with Save the Children in Northern Ireland.

Duncan Morrow is Chief Executive Officer of the Community Relations Council in Northern Ireland.

Shaun Mulvenna is the winner of the 2007 Young Life and Times essay-writing competition. He was 16 years old at the time. Shaun lives in County Antrim, Northern Ireland.

Ruth Sinclair is Director of the National Children's Bureau Northern Ireland.

Alex Tennant is Head of Policy and Research at Save the Children in Northern Ireland.

Acknowledgements

The Young Life and Times project is a team effort. As well as the book editors, the management group includes two ARK colleagues, Katrina Lloyd and Lizanne Dowds, and Ed Cairns from the School of Psychology, University of Ulster. We appreciate their continued support. We are also grateful for the support from Mike McCool who provides significant technical assistance in managing both the YLT survey and YLT as an online research resource, and for the administrative and secretarial support from Ann Marie Dorrity and Shonagh Higgenbotham.

The production of this volume would not be possible without the many generous funders who have supported the YLT survey since its inception, including the Economic and Social Research Council; Save the Children; the EU Programme for Peace and Reconciliation in Northern Ireland and the Border Region of Ireland 2000–04, Measure 2:1 – Reconciliation for Sustainable Peace; the Electoral Commission and the Nuffield Foundation. In particular, we would like to acknowledge the support of the Carnegie UK Trust, which made this book possible.

We would also like to acknowledge the support given by Department for Social Development and by Inland Revenue in providing the sample for the YLT survey.

Most importantly, we appreciate the time and effort taken by all the 16-year olds who responded to the survey.

CHAPTER 1

Shared or scared? Attitudes to community relations among young people 2003–7

Duncan Morrow

The challenge of building better community relations in Northern Ireland

Community division remains the great structuring principle of Northern Ireland. While there are measurable exceptions, religious tradition, tied more loosely to religious observance, remains by far the best predictor of political orientation and behaviour, with the important exception of people, mostly arrived within the last generation, who have allegiances and cultural identity with other places. The nexus between religion, economics and politics, established in the long journey from plantation to partition, remains tightly woven and institutionalised through political parties; key formative institutions like schools, residence; cultural monoliths like Orangism and Gaelic sport, and more fundamental everyday matters like friendship, kinship and marriage. Only the workplace, the integrated school and the shopping centre can claim to have pierced the glass curtain, and even here there are variations of class, location, and occupation. In the shadow of British/Irish colonial politics, the inherited consequence has been the emergence of people who regard each other with profound suspicion often on the basis of real and experienced exclusion, threat and violence.

The formal origin of 'community relations work' in Northern Ireland was in a belated official recognition by the Unionist government that the system was collapsing under the weight of polarisation along Protestant/Catholic lines. The emergence of persistent violence, mass flight and expulsions in working class communities in many locations between 1969 and 1972 led the Stormont

1

government to establish a new Department of State and a Commission charged with reducing social tension. In an attempt to generate mechanisms for the articulation of community grievances and goals, the Commission adopted a proactive approach to community development in many neighbourhoods.

The result fuelled the rise of articulate and active community organisations, which grew up over time into a recognised 'sector' largely designed to articulate social and economic grievances on a highly localised and politically segregated model. For as long as the constitutional question was set aside, this model allowed for the emergence of coalitions of interest along a variety of social and political issues and of a capable level of community leadership beyond – although often closely linked to – political parties and paramilitary formations. What it did not do, was to generate a critical mass of activists aspiring to sharing or a new inter-community embrace.

Republican, and even some less radical nationalist critics of community relations attacked it on three fronts:

- *Accepting the British analysis*: a lazy acceptance of a 'two traditions' hypothesis which failed accurately to articulate the causal role of British colonialism and the British state in embedding and developing sectarianism.
- *Blame the community*: accepting a diagnosis of violence at the point of visibility, tending to blame violence directly on those carrying it out rather than seeing working class violence as a reactive phenomenon to an institutionally sectarianised society.
- *The harmony agenda*: a willingness to accept discrimination and injustice rather than to confront the need for measurable redistribution and fairness.

Unionists were usually suspicious on other grounds:

- *A Trojan horse*: through a civil rights based dialogue, disarming the Unionist community in the face of confident nationalist assertions of discrimination and exclusion.
- *Abandonment*: community relations was part of a general distancing of the British state from its proper role of defending its loyal citizens against a criminal insurgency.
- *Morally dubious*: including paramilitaries and murderers in a false equality with the servants and supporters of the law.

Whatever the reservations, and they were deeply rooted in the political assumptions of all sides, the decisions to bring outright violence to an end and to negotiate for a new basis of shared inter-community government in the mid 1990s, confronted all parties with the contradictions of sharing government and continuing to conduct community relations on the basis of undimmed hostility. Whatever the official ideology, the reality of the political structure emerging from the Good Friday Agreement of 1998 was of two-community politics. Sharing the future across this division was, as the saying goes, 'the new black'.

It is hard to describe any state that is rooted in the identity of one part of the community and explicitly over and against the identity of the remainder of the population as anything other than sectarian. Unfortunately, one of its more lasting elements was an opposition equally unable to provide a transcendent space for all. The difficulties in translating the high aspirations of the Good Friday Agreement into practice stemmed directly from the contradictions of opposing political aspirations and the implications of peace without victory. Building a shared future was nobody's primary aspiration but it was the automatic corollary of the peace declarations. Explicitly or implicitly, the crucial test of the quality of peace was the safety and security it brought to relations across the traditional community divide.

In the absence of victory, it is clear that this is the one relationship which has the potential to destroy inter-community government. Problematically, clearing up the issues which have generated separated political/religious/cultural 'communities' is a much more complex and long term task than designing a viable or semi-viable constitution. It may be a cliché, but Northern Ireland proves beyond doubt that reconciliation is not an event. Alongside a new deal on political power and institutions comes a new deal on law and order (policing, the monopoly of violence and the end to private, paramilitary and all non-state armies), redress for structural economic and social inequalities and a commitment to erode those structures and cultural forces which are designed to protect people from one another rather than meet one another as partners. Each of these in their turn has the capacity to create new antagonism. In a society built on antagonism, the decision to pursue a shared future is a decision which alters everything.

The story of the peace process after 1998 illustrates just how hard the political leadership of Northern Ireland found it to sign up to the full consequences of peace building. Early attempts to establish a working executive fell after a matter of months. The IRA was clearly unwilling to decommission its arsenal while the Ulster Unionists struggled to defend themselves against the allegation of a sell out from without and within their own party. Eventually, in October 2002, the inter-party Executive collapsed when the police raided Sinn Féin's offices in Stormont in pursuit of an alleged spy ring.

Only the persistent, sometimes desperate, commitment of the British, Irish and allied governments to a new deal which would offer some end to the endless division of Northern Ireland kept the broader political process intact. The other critical element in the continuity of the peace process was the stoic reaction of the people. While it was hard to discern any powerful dynamic towards sharing, and indeed the elections of 2003 seemed at one level to suggest a greater polarisation than ever, there was no discernable appetite for any return to violence.

The period covered by these five years of the Young Life and Times (YLT) surveys have proved to be a period 'between':

- The Good Friday Agreement and St Andrews Agreement.
- One period of inter-community government and another.
- A society which still treated paramilitaries as normal to one in which decommissioning took place and there was a new agreement around policing.

It was therefore also a period of contradictory moments: paramilitary violence declined but the McCartney case* showed that some were still immune to detection; support for the forces of law and order began to solidify but there was increasing evidence of dirty tricks in state behaviour in the past; troop levels reduced but troops returned to the streets over major parading divisions.

The surveys provide significant and important evidence of the underlying approaches of young people to one another and of the state of inter-community relations at this time. Above all, in the long saga that is reconciliation, they reflect the challenges and 'baggage' of the first 'shared future' political generation.

---

* Robert McCartney was murdered outside a city centre bar in Belfast in on 30 January 2005. His sisters and his partner suspected IRA involvement in the murder, and subsequent cover-up and intimidation of witnesses of this incident. They started a very public campaign to encourage witnesses to come forward, which took them to Westminster and the White House. This campaign gained them both strong support and opposition. The IRA has repeatedly denied any involvement in Robert McCartney's murder. To date no-one has been convicted for this crime.

The legacy of violence and the pattern of fear

Most of the older generation behave negatively towards people from different backgrounds. I hope that my generation behave more naturally and openly to different people and cultures.

(Comment from a YLT respondent, 2006)

Anyone reading the community relations data from the YLT surveys is confronted by the long length of the shadow of violence. The paramilitary ceasefires may have been a decade old, but the proportions of young people reporting an ongoing and direct impact on their lives in 2004 was considerable (Table 1.1):

[handwritten annotation: ↓ high ↓ but how? clok friend detuned]

Table 1.1   Respondents reporting experiences of violence

	%
Have you ever been threatened by a paramilitary group?	8
Has a member of your family or close friend in your community ever had to move house because of intimidation?	16
Has a member of your family's or a close friend's home ever been damaged in a bomb?	14
Has a member of your family or a close friend in your community ever been injured due to a sectarian attack?	30
Has a member of your family or a close friend ever been threatened by paramilitaries?	28
Has there been any time in the last year when you felt intimidated or threatened because people were wearing certain football strips?	28
Has there been any time in the last year when you were intimidated or threatened by loyalist murals, kerb painting or flags?	35
Has there been any time in the last year when you were intimidated or threatened by republican murals, kerb painting or flags?	26

Source: YLT survey 2004   *[handwritten: – need to compare this with PSE]*

Direct threat by paramilitaries remained a measurable factor for many young people in 2004. While it is not possible from Table 1.1 to ascertain the degree or level of any threat, the data confirm that conflict was not merely a political reality but an inter-generational and socially structuring experience. Significantly, religious background played no role in this experience, and males were only slightly more likely than females to have been affected.

The consequences of bombing and intimidation continue to have clear community and inter-generational effects. Given the sharp decline in the number of bomb attacks in Northern Ireland after the Omagh bomb in 1998, and the extent of residential segregation resulting from intimidation measured elsewhere, we can speculate that the levels of response to these questions are, to some degree, tied to the experiences of previous generations. But as political and civic society struggles to find a mechanism to explore the truth about conflict and violence, the unmistakable message of YLT is of the extent to which these experiences have been part of private everyday life and immediate memory.

To some degree, the issue of murals and street painting points to an even more pervasive, if possibly less acute, sense of threat. The global responses to questions about such intimidation mask sharper inter-community differentials. Indeed in 2004, 55 per cent of Catholics reported being intimidated by loyalist murals while 36 per cent of Protestants responded similarly to republican displays. We can only speculate on the long-run impact of these kinds of images, but we should be in no doubt that the message of hostility, antagonism and cultural exclusivism has permeated broadly and deeply across society even in the 'peace process generation'.

Political debates tend to return to 'causes', but young people live among the debris of the consequences in which everyone played their part. Having a cause does not allow anyone to avoid responsibility for consequences. Conflict in the North of Ireland has now generated communities which share a formative memory in violence, but are absolutely divided about where threat comes from. If 'dealing with the past' means unpicking the legacy of trauma and violence, any process of truth recovery will inevitably mean that those seeking acknowledgement about their experience of intimidation from outside will also be confronted with evidence of the intimidation of others from inside. In inter-community terms, violence and intimidation emanated in both directions, with no clear identification of consistency about who was the victim and who the perpetrator, only evidence of shockingly widespread experiences of both. In the absence of victory, where one party may be more able to shape and control the flow of information, truth recovery will be a process of accusation as much as of vindication for both communities.

Celebrating diversity?

I don't think people should care what colour or religion a person is as we are all the same and no one deserves to be discriminated against and no one has the right to discriminate against another person.

(Comment from a YLT respondent, 2006)

The 'nought-ies' may go down in the history of the North of Ireland as both the decade of the peace process and the decade where inter-ethnic diversity became a reality for the first time. Having supplied the melting pots of Boston, Sydney and London for generations, peace and prosperity generated a new phenomenon – people choosing to move to Northern Ireland. Both of these radical changes are reflected in the YLT surveys.

In spite of the ups and downs of the peace process, young people remained optimistic. Even within their own lives, the respondents could identify improvements in both inter-community and inter-ethnic relations, reflected across both religion and gender (Table 1.2).

Table 1.2 Would you say that relations between Protestants and Catholics are better than they were five years ago?

	2003	2004	2005	2006	2007
Better	41	48	43	46	61
Worse	17	16	12	11	8
About the same	37	32	34	33	27

Source: YLT surveys 2003–7

[handwritten annotation: What are longer term trends?]

Even in the absence of political agreement, this provides supporting evidence of the ongoing experience of better relationships on the ground throughout the 'peace process'. While a steady proportion of young people could identify improvement, there is a more consistent trend away from pessimism by 2006. In 2007, there was a marked increase in optimism, no doubt related to the reinstatement of the Executive earlier that year. Perhaps surprisingly, each year a higher proportion of males were optimistic than was the case for females (e.g. 66% and 57% respectively in 2007). Similarly a consistently higher proportion of Catholics could identify improvement than among their Protestant counterparts, or among those with no religion. Interestingly, those who had no religious identity were marginally more pessimistic than those identifying as Catholic of Protestant (see Table 1.3). However, by 2007, less than eight per cent of young people from all religious backgrounds thought that things had got worse.

Table 1.3 Would you say that relations between Protestants and Catholics are better than they were five years ago? By religious background

	%		
	Catholic	*Protestant*	*None*
Better	70	58	54
Worse	5	8	12
About the same	23	30	25

Source: YLT survey 2007

Movement towards tolerance and openness in Northern Ireland still takes place in the face of perceived social and peer pressure against overly intimate inter-community or inter-ethnic relations. Unsurprisingly, families continue to exercise by far the strongest influence on young people, as Table 1.4 shows.

Table 1.4 What do you think has been the most important influence on your views about the other religious community?

	%			
	2003	*2004*	*2005*	*2007*
Your church	6	10	7	5
Your family	47	46	43	40
Your school	9	8	10	9
Your friends	21	16	19	15
Other	13	6	4	6

Source: YLT surveys 2003–5, 2007

The influence of friends was slightly stronger for males than females, whereas the influence of school appeared stronger for females. Churches and *is this stat sig?*

friends appear to have slightly more influence on Protestants than Catholics, whereas the influence of school was stronger for Catholics.

The consequences of these complex, and possibly reinforcing, influences were reflected in some apparent contradictions between personal attitudes and assumptions made about others on the actions of young people. Asked about their own attitudes towards marriage to people of a different religion or of different ethnic origin, most young people professed themselves to be open-minded (Table 1.5).

Table 1.5 Would you *personally* mind or not mind if a close relative were to marry someone . . . By survey year

	%						
	. . . of a different religion				. . . of a different race or ethnic origin		
	2003	*2004*	*2005*	*2006*	*2004*	*2005*	*2006*
Mind a lot	7	7	8	6	6	5	7
Mind a little	20	21	13	18	18	16	17
Not mind	71	67	70	69	72	70	68

Source: YLT surveys 2003–6

Importantly, more than three-quarters of Catholic respondents indicated complete openness to 'mixed' relationships whether on a religious or inter-ethnic basis. Among Protestants, the figure fell to approximately 60 per cent. Without further interrogation of these responses, we can only speculate about the explanations and context of these attitudinal differences. However, it does suggest that suspicion of inter-community interaction remains measurably stronger for young Protestants.

When asked about the attitudes of the surrounding community, however, both Catholics and Protestant young people were aware of significant concerns about the acceptability of exogamy (Table 1.6).

Once more there was a measurable difference between the concerns of Catholics (among whom only 14–17%, depending on the survey year, thought that most people would mind a lot) and young Protestants (where between 22–27% registered a strong concern). The starkly different responses of young people responding about themselves and the society around them may

Table 1.6 Do you think that *most people* in Northern Ireland would mind if one of their close relatives were to marry someone . . . By survey year

	%						
	. . . *of a different religion*				. . . *of a different race or ethnic origin*		
	2003	*2004*	*2005*	*2006*	*2004*	*2005*	*2006*
Mind a lot	27	24	20	18	22	18	19
Mind a little	48	49	45	48	46	43	45
Not mind	19	19	21	22	22	23	24

Source: YLT surveys 2003–6

represent an ongoing awareness of the cultural climate in which relationships take place. This may in itself influence outcomes even in this generation. Alternatively it may presage the arrival of a more globally open and cosmopolitan approach. Support for either view can be gathered from responses to other questions. Table 1.7, for example, shows respondents' feelings towards people from minority ethnic backgrounds.

Table 1.7 How favourable or unfavourable do you feel about people from minority ethnic communities?

	%			
	2004	*2005*	*2006*	*2007*
Very favourable	13	10	12	13
Favourable	26	18	23	21
Neither favourable nor unfavourable	48	51	48	52
Unfavourable	5	5	6	4
Very unfavourable	2	3	2	2
Don't know	6	7	8	9

Source: YLT surveys 2004–7

In this case there were only marginal variations between people of different religious backgrounds, but some evidence that females were more positive than males. The same broad pattern of responses was evident when asked about underlying attitudes to interaction between people of different ethnic origin (Table 1.8):

Table 1.8 In relation to colour and ethnicity I prefer to stick to people of my own kind

	%
Strongly agree	3
Agree	9
Neither agree nor disagree	26
Disagree	30
Strongly disagree	30

Source: YLT survey 2007

The figures add up to a complex picture. On the one hand, it is clear that the exclusive single-culture community is favoured by only a small minority. On the other, only slightly more than 50 per cent were committed to interaction, suggesting that issues of social cohesion around matters of race and ethnicity may be subject to the same complicated patterns of exclusion and embrace that have characterised the rest of Ireland and the United Kingdom. The relative newness of the issue for a generation in Northern Ireland makes these questions an important source of information about evolving integration into the future.

In coming to Northern Ireland, newcomers arrive in a place where organisational and residential separation between Catholics and Protestants are already stark and where a consciousness of 'difference' focussed on the monolithic structure of religious, political and cultural opposition is powerful. Over the years, YLT surveys have continued to ask young people about their attitudes to some of the starkest elements of that separate development – residence, education and work.

Violence in the 1970s led to a sharp increase in the number of places which were understood as the exclusive residential preserve of one group. While the pace of separation may have slowed down in later decades, the trend has not been reversed. In spite of this, YLT confirmed the consistent finding that a clear majority continue to indicate a preference for mixed-religion neighbourhoods (Table 1.9):

Table 1.9 If you had your choice, would you prefer to live in a neighbourhood with people of only your own religion, or in a mixed-religion neighbourhood? By survey year

	%				
	2003	*2004*	*2005*	*2006*	*2007*
Own religion only	35	36	29	29	23
Mixed-religion neighbourhood	53	52	56	53	62

Source: YLT surveys 2003–7

Over the period, the proportions favouring mixed-religion neighbourhoods have remained remarkably constant. If there has been a trend, it is in a small reduction of those who actively favoured single identity neighbourhoods. In the face of permanent inter-community antagonism and political competition, the fact that a majority continue to believe in mixed-religion neighbourhoods is a small kind of triumph. On the other hand, the very notion of single religion neighbourhoods should be anathema in most democratic countries, and would shock in the United Kingdom or Ireland if it referred to race and ethnicity or was applied to other social issues like sexuality. The fact that around one quarter of the young population continues to prefer effective residential apartheid presents serious long-term challenges. In political terms, a determined minority of this size can create obstacles to integration, making life difficult for any small incoming minority and generating a common sense that integrated living will be actively opposed.

Even more than residential neighbourhoods, schools continue to operate in parallel for Catholics and Protestants. In spite of the impressive rise of intentionally integrated schools, more than 90 per cent of Catholic and Protestant young people are educated separately to secondary level. The YLT surveys suggest that there is no social consensus on this issue and that neither systematic integration nor the notion of permanently separated schools command overwhelming support, as Table 1.10 shows.

The central significance which the Roman Catholic Church attaches to church schooling and/or the central significance of Gaelic games may account for the greater proportion of Catholics supporting single-religion education. Whatever the case, it is significant that Protestants appear to attach greater importance to single-identity housing while Catholic interest in diversity is

Table 1.10   Would you prefer a school with children only of your own religion or a mixed-religion school?

			%		
	2003	*2004*	*2005*	*2006*	*2007*
Own religion only	42	47	43	43	40
Mixed-religion school	48	43	45	43	49

Source: YLT surveys 2003–7

focussed more on education. It is a moot point which has the greater impact on securing distinctive community identity.

Evidence on attitudes to the workplace, on the other hand, suggests that the issue of separation no longer plays any serious role in young people's expectations (Table 1.11).

Table 1.11   Would you prefer a workplace with people of your own religion or in a mixed-religion workplace?

	2003	*2004*	*2005*	*2006*	*2007*
Own religion only	17	18	15	12	13
Mixed-religion workplace	71	67	70	70	73

Source: YLT surveys 2003–7

Taken together, evidence on attitudes to residence, education and the workplace suggest that there was remarkably little substantive change in young people's expectations or views between 2003 and 2007. Clearly these issues have not gone away and ambivalence about both sharing and separation is evident in all cases except in the workplace. On the one hand this may be due to the success of decades of equal opportunities policies. On the other it may be that separation is reserved for the more intimate spheres of young people's lives – living, learning and playing – while contact is understood as essential for the necessary but more regulated interactions of paid work.

A new beginning?

I feel that they should keep trying to bring the communities together but feel that it is not working at this time.

(Comment from a YLT respondent, 2006)

It may, of course, be dangerous to read too much about future trends into these surveys. Few professional observers would have predicted in 1997 that political negotiations would produce a working coalition between the Democratic Unionist Party (DUP) and Sinn Féin. Undoubtedly, the mood among young people in Northern Ireland between 2003 and 2007 remained one of profound realism, shaped by years of hostility and a public wrangling over political co-operation. Ultimately, most young people appeared to look at the past as the best predictor of the future.

Table 1.12   Will religion always make a difference to the way people feel about each other in Northern Ireland?

	2003	2004	2005	2006	2007
Yes	86	86	84	78	81
No	8	8	10	10	11

Source: YLT surveys 2003–7

While there were some marginal differences between females and males and between Protestants, Catholics and people of no religion, more than three quarters of people in every category were resigned to the persistence of ongoing issues around religion. It would be wrong, however, to characterise this realism as terminally pessimistic. Set alongside previous evidence that relations had improved over the last five years (see Table 1.3), there was some evidence of ongoing expectation of further progress in building better relationships in the years to come (Table 1.13).

In each of the survey years, males were generally more optimistic than their female counterparts. However, there was a stronger correlation with religious background, with Catholics markedly more hopeful than either Protestants or people declaring no religion (Figure 1.1).

Were this to happen in practice, this would represent a continuous gap between Catholic and Protestant hopes and fears lasting over a full decade of

Table 1.13 In 5 years time, do you think relations between Protestants and Catholics will be better than now, worse than now or about the same? By survey year

	%				
	2003	*2004*	*2005*	*2006*	*2007*
Better	36	39	36	39	49
Worse	15	14	13	12	5
About the same	42	40	38	39	39

Source: YLT surveys 2003–7

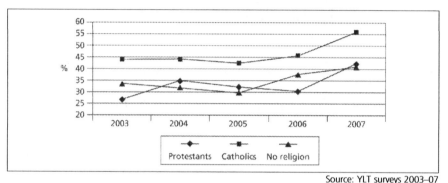

Source: YLT surveys 2003–07

Figure 1.1 Respondents saying that, in 5 years time, relations between Protestants and Catholics will be *better* than now. By survey year and religious background

peace building. While the differences are not so enormous as to be contradictory, we can speculate on the impact of a decade of what feels like continual progress on one side of a political and cultural division against the greater reticence on the other. In the light of the momentous political events of 2007, it will be important to continue to track these attitudes following the actual achievement of devolved partnership government and to assess their impact.

Conclusions

The children who first entered primary school on 1 September 1994 did so on the day after the IRA announced its first ceasefire. On 30 June 2008, those still in school will complete their secondary education. These are truly the children of the peace process years.

They and their siblings were born into a society in conflict and they enter adulthood in a society with stable political structures. The YLT surveys 2003–7 reflect an ambivalent generation. The legacy of inter-community conflict continues to give special relevance to the notion of Catholic and Protestant even in a secular age. The surveys reflect young people who have come to terms with the inherited normality of distinguishing people on a 'community' basis alongside a persistent sense that the present is preferable to the past and the future might just be better than the present.

What the surveys do not show is that Northern Ireland's inter-community issues are resolved. While the new voters of the next decade have grown up in a world where ethnic minorities are a real part of their own experience, and where the dream of progress towards an widely acceptable political framework survived through a series of shocks, this is not a generation which has closed the book on past hurts or divisions or finally found ease with diversity. Negotiating a new deal on safety, housing, education and even personal relationships remains work in progress.

This is not yet a revolutionary generation in 1960s-like revolt. But there is evidence of a slow evolution, away from an expectation of eternal war, to one of negotiated pluralism. Young people's attitudes reflected in the surveys, and especially in the more personal comments collected with them, convey both a frustration with the impasse of community division and a tacit understanding of the parameters within which people from different backgrounds live. On the other hand this is a generation expectant of change. It is this expectation which gives them its political power, impacting directly on the direction of politicians and political plans.

If YLT shows anything it is that living with and resolving ambivalence – between the impossibility of the past and the strangeness of any other future – may well be the agenda for Northern Ireland for the next decade. There is no expectation among young people that change will be rapid. Community relations issues will remain a critical test for governments and leaders for some years yet. As one of the 2006 YLT respondents put it: 'Community relations are improving, but gradually and not by much'.

CHAPTER 2

Adolescent mental health in Northern Ireland: empirical evidence from the Young Life and Times survey

Katrina Lloyd, Ed Cairns, Claire Doherty and Kate Ellis

Introduction

In Northern Ireland over the last decade a relatively low-key debate has been ongoing as to what impact (if any) the ending of political violence has had on the mental health of the population in general and on young people in particular. In this chapter we will attempt to add some empirical evidence to this debate where adolescents are concerned. We will do this by analysing data made available from the Young Life and Times (YLT) surveys from 2004 to 2006.

Post-conflict Northern Ireland and adolescent mental health

While young people in Northern Ireland were not exposed to political violence to the same extent as children caught up in all out war, many children did experience such things as rioting or witnessing a shooting or a bomb explosion. At the same time, contemporary studies suggested that the *majority* of children and young people in Northern Ireland did not suffer any serious psychological consequences as a result of the ongoing political violence (a minority of course suffered terribly). There was evidence however linking variations in levels of anti-social behaviour to variations in levels of political violence (Muldoon and Trew, 2000).

Despite the ending of most political violence, since the ceasefires of the 1990s there has been a strong belief that, if anything, adolescent mental health levels in Northern Ireland have deteriorated rather than improved. For example, there have been concerns voiced in the press and elsewhere about the general level of mental health in Northern Ireland. Certainly it would appear that over the last 30 years suicide rates in Northern Ireland have been increasing. What is more, over the period 1983–2001 suicide rates have been highest in the youngest age bands (16–24 and 25–34 years).

What has caught the public's attention is not just the absolute number of suicides but the fact that suicide rates in Northern Ireland have been rising steeply at least since 1998. The most dramatic increases have been largely confined to the city of Belfast and even then only to certain parts of Belfast, in particular North and West Belfast.

All this is borne out by the available statistics, which show that between 1998 and 2004 Northern Ireland had the second highest increase in all suicides (22%) in the United Kingdom (UK) (see Brock et al., 2006, for more details). Further, in Northern Ireland, both Belfast North and Belfast West had suicide rates over 50 per cent higher than the UK rate. More perplexing is the fact that in Belfast North the male suicide rate more than doubled and in Belfast West there was a 94 per cent increase in this period. In comparison, Belfast East and Belfast South had lower rates compared to the UK as a whole (25–49% lower than the UK rate).

Despite the media interest, there has been comparatively little academic research, particularly prospective research into the problem of suicide among young people in Northern Ireland and Belfast in particular. In the most recent of a handful of academic studies to look at the problem in relation to the political violence that has just ended in Northern Ireland, McGowan et al. (2005) concluded that 'the Troubles' possibly increased social cohesion, which in turn protected individuals from suicide. However the authors also note that even the finding of an inverse correlation between suicides and death due to the political violence does not necessarily mean that the two are causally related.

Notwithstanding these obvious pointers to the importance of mental health among young adults, this age group has largely been neglected in terms of actual research. For this reason, in 2004, the YLT survey began to include a number of questions designed to measure mental health levels among its adolescent participants.

In this chapter we will first examine the data from the YLT survey conducted in 2004 in an attempt to highlight the main sources of stress for adolescents in Northern Ireland. In the second part of our chapter we will focus on cumulative data from the three YLT surveys conducted in 2004, 2005 and 2006. These data will be used in an attempt to determine if adolescent mental health levels are, as the public fear, worsening over time in post-violence Northern Ireland.

The evidence

In all the YLT surveys reported here the procedures and measures were approximately the same. A letter containing the questionnaire and a pre-stamped return envelope were posted out to all eligible 16-year olds. Each letter contained an ID number (with a check letter) for the individual participant. All documentation and information for the surveys was processed by an independent research organisation. Respondents were given the choice of three methods of completing the questionnaire: by phone, on-line, or by completing the paper questionnaire and posting it back using the pre-stamped envelope (almost all chose this latter method).

All questionnaires contained the 12-item General Health Questionnaire (GHQ12), designed to identify short-term changes in mental health, a measure of mental health which has been widely used in adult surveys in Northern Ireland. The GHQ12 is a screening instrument for non-psychotic psychiatric disorder and is based on answers to questions about 12 symptoms such as concentration, sleep-loss due to worry, anxiety, loss of confidence and general happiness. This questionnaire has been found to have satisfactory reliability and validity for 16-year olds in the United Kingdom (Stafford, Jackson and Banks, 1980) and has been shown to be reliable and valid amongst community samples in Northern Ireland (Cairns et al., 1991).

GHQ12

1. Sources of stress

In this section we first want to determine just how many young people could be said to be 'psychologically distressed' and then to explore the principal causes of their stress. To do this we used data from the YLT survey conducted in 2004. A total of 1,983 questionnaires were sent out, 824 were returned completed, a response rate of 42 per cent. Of these, 42 per cent were males and 58 per cent females, the majority of whom designated themselves as white (97%) and reported that they had lived ten or more years in Northern Ireland (97%). Also 39 per cent indicated that they saw themselves as 'part of the Protestant community', 44 per cent as 'part of the Catholic community' while a further 17 per cent said they saw themselves as 'neither'.

There are various ways to score the GHQ12. In this study we used what is known as the 'scale score' which involves taking people's answers to the 12 questions and adding up the number of times the person placed themselves in either the fairly stressed or highly stressed category. Doing this, the 'worst' possible score is 12 – this indicates that the young person responded negatively to every one of the 12 questions. On the other hand the 'best' level of psychological well-being is a score of zero, indicating the individual unusual stress levels in response to any of the 12 questions.

In our first set of analyses we will adhere to the convention of focusing on those people who responded at the negative end of the scale and did so in response to four or more of the questions on the GHQ12 (the 'caseness' method). A score of four or more is often taken to indicate a level of psychological distress that could be of clinical significance, meaning that a young person scoring four or more would need to be referred to a specialist in the field of mental health for a more detailed investigation.

A general indication of the overall mental health levels of our 16-year old sample in 2004 can be obtained by looking at the scores of the 791 young people who completed the GHQ12. In total 24 per cent scored four or more suggesting that about one quarter of the sample were suffering enough to be considered to be 'psychological distressed' and therefore in need of further investigation. Further, it is clear that more females (30%) than males (16%) fell into the psychologically distressed category. This gender difference in stress levels is clearly not just confined to answers given to the GHQ12 but can also be seen in the responses to the simple question 'How often do you get stressed?' (Table 2.1). In response to this question some 47 per cent of male respondents said they rarely or never got stressed while only 25 per cent of females responded in the same way.

What do 16-year-olds worry about?

Psychological distress can result from the circumstances we find ourselves in at any given time in our lives. To explore this idea the young people who took

Table 2.1   How often do you get stressed?

	%	
	Male	*Female*
Very often	6	12
Often	14	24
Sometimes	33	39
Rarely	39	21
Never	8	4

part in the YLT survey were invited to freely respond to the question 'What makes you stressed?' In all, 77 per cent of participants took the trouble to answer this question. To simplify the analyses we sorted all the answers into eight categories (Table 2.2). The responses to this question make it obvious that schoolwork/exams was easily the most frequently mentioned stressor and that this was equally true for both sexes.

Table 2.2   What makes you stressed?

	%		
	Males	*Females*	*All*
School work/exams	56	79	70
Family problems	19	30	26
Financial problems/work	19	13	15
Being under pressure	7	18	12
Life in general/worrying	5	10	8
Problems with friends	13	12	12
Relationship problems	6	10	8
Health problems	1	5	3

We had anticipated that school might be an important factor and therefore had a key question about life at school – 'How often do you feel pressured by schoolwork?' In all 75 per cent said that they had felt pressured by schoolwork at least 'sometimes', with over one quarter saying this happened 'often' or 'always' (Table 2.3). Again these results did not differ between the sexes.

Table 2.3 And to what extent does this statement apply to your experience of school: I felt pressured by the school work I had to do

	%		
	Males	*Females*	*All*
Always	5	5	5
Often	20	22	21
Sometimes	46	51	49
Rarely	22	18	20
Never	7	4	5

Because it is possible that feeling pressured by schoolwork is related to the type of school attended we next looked at the answers to this question given by those who were at secondary school compared to those at grammar school.* We found there were no differences where males were concerned but did find that young women at grammar school were more likely to say they were 'always' or 'often' pressured at school compared to those at secondary school (Table 2.4).

Table 2.4 Respondents feeling pressured by schoolwork: secondary and grammar school students compared

Gender		%		
		Always or often	*Sometimes*	*Rarely or never*
Male	Grammar	24	49	27
	Secondary	26	47	27
Female	Grammar	34	47	18
	Secondary	20	54	26

Despite this gender difference, when we looked to see if being pressured at school was related to levels of psychological distress we found that it was and

---

* At the time of the survey Northern Ireland had a selective secondary school system with more academic grammar schools and less academic secondary schools.

that this was equally true for boys and for girls. As Table 2.5 shows, more young people could be considered to be psychologically distressed among those who said they were 'always' or 'often' pressured at school, compared to those who said they felt 'sometimes' pressured and those who answered 'rarely' or 'never'. Among females the rate doubled but among males the increase was almost treble.

Table 2.5   Pressured by schoolwork and levels of psychological distress

Gender	Stressed by school work	Psychologically distressed (%)
Male	Always or often	32
	Sometimes	8
	Rarely or never	13
Female	Always or often	45
	Sometimes	23
	Rarely or never	26

2. Adolescents' stress levels 2004–06

In an attempt to examine adolescent stress levels in Northern Ireland over time we examined the data from all those young people who responded to the YLT surveys in the years 2004–2006. In total, over the three years there were 2,415 participants (1,005 were male and 1,402 were female) from across Northern Ireland. The response rates from 2004–2006 were 42 per cent, 40 per cent and 39 per cent respectively.

Responses to the GHQ12 were based on a 4-point scale (not at all, less than usual, no more than usual, much more than usual) and were scored using the 'Likert scoring' method (0, 1, 2, 3). A score of 3 would mean that someone had said that they not only experienced a particular symptom in the last month, but that they had experienced it 'much more than usual'. The scores from each question on the GHQ12 were then summed to give total scores that ranged from 0–36. Higher total scores reflect *poorer* psychological well-being or mental health (Goldberg, 1978).

Examination of the mean score on the GHQ12 revealed that, over the years 2004 to 2006, there was a small but statistically significant decrease in GHQ12 scores (F (2, 1816)=3.60, $p<0.05$). Overall, average scores on the GHQ12 were higher in 2004 (10.34) than in 2005 (9.64) and 2006 (9.51) (Figure 2.1). Incidentally this is not an artefact due to the way the GHQ12 has been scored. If the 'caseness' method is used the results also indicate improving levels of mental health with 24 per cent, 21 per cent and 20 per cent of the sample in each of the years 2004, 2005 and 2006 respectively falling into the 'psychologically distressed' category as defined above. Most importantly in the present context, the year in which the survey was undertaken showed no statistically significant interaction with other important variables such as gender, denomination or whether the young person lived in a city, a town, the suburbs or in the country or in a village. This means that this yearly decline in GHQ scores applied to all who took part regardless of their gender, religion or where they lived. As Figure 2.1 shows, in all three survey years females had higher mean scores, reflecting poorer psychological wellbeing.

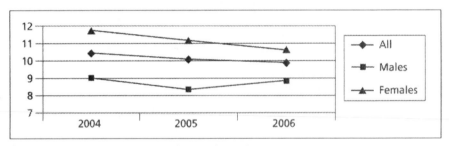

Figure 2.1   GHQ12 mean score by gender and YLT survey year

To summarise therefore, contrary to expectations, based on the evidence from the 2004–2006 YLT surveys, there is evidence of a small but steady *improvement* in mental health among Northern Irish 16-year olds.

Discussion

Because no other recent survey has comprehensively looked at mental health in this age group it is difficult to say with any certainty whether the levels of psychological distress reported here for 16-year-olds in Northern Ireland in 2004, are unusually high or not. The 2001 Northern Ireland Health and Social Wellbeing survey (NISRA, 2001) did include the GHQ12 questionnaire. However, among the random sample of 5,025 adults that completed the survey, the number of 16-year olds was relatively small (n = 92). Seventy-five 16-year olds completed all 12 GHQ12 questions in this survey. Among these respondents, 18 per cent had a GHQ12 score of four or higher. The rates of psychological distress in the YLT surveys are also slightly higher than those from a comparable adult sample in Northern Ireland where of those sampled in 2001, 20 per cent had a score of four or more on the GHQ12 (Murphy and Lloyd, 2007). One possible explanation for this result could be the fact that, as earlier research in Northern Ireland has shown, as young people leave school their mental health tends to improve (Cairns et al., 1991). This may indicate that psychological distress at 16 years is, at least for most young people, transient. This would also fit with our finding that the main stressor for 16-year olds is schoolwork (Cairns and Lloyd, 2005).

It is also encouraging to see that levels of psychological distress among young people in Northern Ireland may be beginning to fall. Corroborating evidence for improvements in mental health levels in Northern Ireland comes from the results of two random sample surveys of adults. The first, carried out in 1997, indicated that 21.3 per cent of those sampled could be considered to be 'psychological distressed' (O'Reilly and Stevenson, 2003). However, when a comparable survey was carried out in 2001 this figure had fallen slightly to 19.7 per cent (Murphy and Lloyd, 2007). It is also of interest to note that the authors of the first survey argued that the rates of psychological distress in Northern Ireland were higher than those in the rest of the UK (O'Reilly and Stevenson, 2003) while Murphy and Lloyd (2007) were able to demonstrate convincingly that in their survey Northern Ireland's results were comparable to the UK average and indeed considerably better than those in Wales.

The difference between the results obtained by O'Reilly and Stevenson (2003) and those reported by Murphy and Lloyd (2007) happen to coincide with the paramilitary ceasefires and the beginning of the ongoing peace process in Northern Ireland. This change in the political climate in Northern Ireland, it could therefore be argued, may account for the differences between 1997 and 2001 for the adult samples and also account for the fall in levels of adolescent psychological distress over the years 2004–2006 reported earlier in this chapter. Certainly this explanation would fit well with the fact that when the young people in the 2004–2006 YLT surveys were asked if relations between Catholics and Protestants in Northern Ireland would be better, worse, or about the same in five years time, results indicate a modest but positive increase in levels of optimism about the future with 36 per cent,

[Handwritten annotations in top margin: "Controlling for other factors – important for my study – how to do it! – regression analysis.)"]

38 per cent and 41 per cent respectively saying that the relations would be 'better'.

Of course the arguments in this chapter are based on relatively few samples and on relatively crude statistics. For example, potential confounding influences such as socio-economic status, demographic environments and family status, which have been found to contribute to adolescent psychological distress (Aneshensel and Sucoff, 1996; Donnelly, 1999; Kessler, 1979) have not been controlled for. In this respect we must await more definite results. If nothing else however, the data presented here underline the value of random samples that are repeated on an annual basis and measure the same variables. Only in this way will changing patterns of responding be detected.

What our results do suggest is that future research should examine the possibility that the last years of education are a particularly stressful period for young people in Northern Ireland, and that for some young people, either because of a combination of environmental or personality factors, this stress may be damaging to their mental health. This is an important finding because, too often commentators forget that even in troubled societies like Northern Ireland, young people still have to face the same problems common to adolescents in the rest of the Western World (Cairns, 1996). Of course this is not to suggest that political violence does not also impact on levels of mental health. Therefore also worth following up is the suggestion that, as the Northern Irish peace process beds in, this in turn may lead to improved mental health perhaps both for adults and young people.

References

Aneshensel, C.S. and Sucoff, C.A. (1996) The Neighbourhood Context of Adolescent Mental Health. *Journal of Health and Social Behaviour*, 37, 293–310.

ARK. Young Life and Times Survey (2005) [computer files]. ARK: www.ark.ac.uk/ylt [Accessed 31 January 2008].

Brock, A., Baker, A., Griffiths, C., Jackson, G., Fegan, G. and Marshall, D. (2006) Suicide Trends and Geographical Variations in the United Kingdom, 1991–2004. *Health Statistics Quarterly* 31, 6–22.

Cairns, E. (1996). *Children and Political Violence*. Oxford: Blackwell.

Cairns, E., McWhirter, L., Barry, R. and Duffy, U. (1991) The Development of Psychological Well-being in Late Adolescence. *Journal of Child Psychology and Psychiatry*, 32: 4, 635–43.

Cairns, E. and Lloyd, K. (2005) *Stress at 16*. ARK Research Update 33. Belfast: ARK. Available online at: www.ark.ac.uk/publications/updates/update33.pdf [Accessed 31 January 2008]

Donnelly, M. (1999) Factors Associated with Depressed Mood among Adolescents in Northern Ireland. *Journal of Community and Applied Social Psychology*, 9: 1, 47–59.

Goldberg, D.P. (1978) *Manual of the General Health Questionnaire*. Windsor: NFER Nelson.

Kessler, R.C. (1979) Stress, Social Status, and Psychological Distress. *Journal of Health and Social Behaviour*, 20: 3, 259–72.

McGowan, I., Hamilton, S., Miller, P. and Kernohan, G. (2005) Contrasting Terrorist-related Deaths with Suicide Trends over 34 years. *Journal of Mental Health*, 14: 4, 399–405.

Muldoon, O.T. and Trew, K. (2000) Social Group Membership and Perceptions of the Self in Northern Irish Children. *International Journal of Behavioral Development*, 24: 3, 330–37.

Murphy, H. and Lloyd, K. (2007) Civil Conflict in Northern Ireland and the Prevalence of Psychiatric Disturbance: A Population Study using the British Household Panel Survey and the Northern Ireland Household Panel Survey across the United Kingdom. *International Journal of Social Psychiatry*, 53: 5, 397–407.

Northern Ireland Statistical and Research Agency (NISRA) (2002) *Northern Ireland Health and Wellbeing Survey*. Belfast: NISRA.

O'Reilly, D. and Stevenson, M. (2003) Mental Health in Northern Ireland: Have 'the Troubles' made it Worse? *Journal of Epidemiological Community Health*, 57: 7, 488–92.

Stafford, E.M., Jackson, P.R., and Banks, M.H. (1980) Employment, Work Involvement and Mental Health in Less Qualified Young People. *Journal of Occupational Psychology*, 53, 291–304.

CHAPTER 3

Tackling bullying in schools: the role of pupil participation

Ruth Sinclair

Introduction

For many young people in Britain and Northern Ireland bullying by their peers, especially in school, is a major concern. There is a growing body of research that examines the extent and nature of bullying among school pupils in Northern Ireland as well as evidence on the help available to young people. Over the years the Young Life and Times (YLT) surveys have contributed considerably to our knowledge on bullying with the inclusion of this topic in the surveys conducted in 1998, 2004 and 2005 (Burns, 2006). The later surveys are particularly useful in providing the perspective of 16-year-olds, who are perhaps better able to give an informed view of what is happening across their school as a whole.

In this chapter I shall briefly note the extent and nature of school bullying in Northern Ireland, drawing on the 2005 and 2006 YLT surveys, together with data from a very recent major research study commissioned by the Department of Education in Northern Ireland (Livesey et al., 2007 – referred to as the DENI study). I will examine what is known about the way in which schools respond to incidents of bullying and finally explore the extent to which schools involve pupils in developing policies to address the issue. This latter topic was a central theme in a study into bullying in primary, post-primary and special schools in Northern Ireland, commissioned by NICCY (The Office of the Northern Ireland Commissioner for Children and Young People) and undertaken by the National Children's Bureau (Schubotz and Sinclair et al., 2006 – referred to here as the NCB NI study).

The NCB NI study, which had both qualitative and quantitative elements, gathered the views of pupils from 14 schools representing the range of school types across Northern Ireland. Principals or senior staff from each school participated in an interview. Interactive group discussions were held with all the pupils in one class in each school, 24 pupils were interviewed individually and 687 pupils completed a short questionnaire. The study deliberately repeated some of the questions used in the YLT surveys (1998, 2005) but was able to elaborate on the survey responses using the input of pupils to the interactive discussion groups. The richness of this qualitative information was strengthened by the use of young researchers within the research team.

Nature and extent of bullying

Being subjected to bullying, especially persistent bullying, can be devastating to children and young people. Many children are made unhappy, their lives blighted by cruelty from their peers. Bullying is the single most common reason for children across the UK to call Childline (Childline, 2007a). In 2006, in Northern Ireland alone over 1,100 children called Childline to seek help because they were being bullied (Childline, 2007b).

Bullying is manifest in different forms and contexts. It is subjective, experienced or felt by the individual. Hence a simple definition is not easy to provide. However, most commentators now agree that bullying:

- Is aggressive behaviour that intentionally hurts or harms another person.
- Is repetitive.
- Involves an imbalance of power between the bullied and the bully.
- Can be physical, verbal or indirect (for example cyber bullying).

The Department for Education in Northern Ireland defines bullying as:

> . . . *deliberately hurtful behaviour, repeated over a period of time, where it is difficult for the victim to defend him or herself.*

> (DENI, 2001: 63)

In 2005 the Northern Ireland Anti-Bullying Forum (NIABF) agreed the following definition of bullying:

> *The repeated use of power by one or more persons intentionally to harm, hurt or adversely affect the rights and needs of another or others.*

> (NIABF, 2005: 2)

There is now good up-to-date evidence of the prevalence of bullying in post-primary schools in Northern Ireland, as reported by pupils themselves, from the 2005 YLT survey and the recent DENI survey (Livesey et al., 2007). As explained in detail in the Appendix, the YLT survey is completed by 16-year olds. The DENI research gathered the views of pupils in Year 6 and Year 9 and reported the findings for each group separately. Here we shall draw on the data from Year 9 pupils as this is most comparable to the YLT surveys. However, the focus on older pupils in this chapter should not hide the uncomfortable fact that in almost all studies primary school pupils are more likely to say they have experienced bullying (Collins et al., 2004; Smith, 2005). When respondents were asked if they had been bullied in the past two months the 2005 YLT and Year 9 DENI respondents gave very similar answers: 30 per cent and 29 per cent respectively said that they had been bullied. However there was considerable divergence in the proportion of respondents who acknowledged they had taken part in bullying: only seven per cent of 16-year-olds in the YLT survey, compared to 21 per cent in the DENI survey, although only three per cent in the latter study admitted to bullying other pupils two or more times in the past two months.

Bullying can take many forms, but all studies report that the most common form of bullying among pupils is name-calling. 'Being called names, made fun of or teased in a hurtful way' was the most common type of bullying experienced by both boys and girls in the DENI survey. The discussion with pupils in the NCB NI study suggests that the issue of name-calling can be subtle, with some pupils, especially boys, finding it difficult to differentiate between what is acceptable as 'only messing about – just a bit of craic' and what is unacceptable as ongoing verbal bullying. In one exchange during the fieldwork for the NCB NI study, one boy said 'slagging is OK; it's funny' but others responded 'It's not funny . . . it causes misery'. It seems important that each school develops a clear understanding of what is acceptable and what is not; an understanding that takes account of the views of pupils. As one young respondent said:

> *Most of the bullying at this school is 'slagging' which most people just put up with – but I don't think they should, because it can escalate.*

'Being called names' is most often linked to real or perceived difference in the characteristics of pupils, such as race, religion, disability or sexual orientation. Both the 2005 and 2006 YLT surveys as well as the DENI survey tell us a great deal about bullying of this sort and its relationship to the attitude of bullies to people with certain characteristics.

While sectarianism is embedded in many parts of Northern Ireland, until very recently the proportion of the population in Northern Ireland from minority ethnic groups was relatively small. According to the 2001 Census, 99 per cent of the population in Northern Ireland are 'white' and fewer than two per cent were born outside the British Isles. However, the last few years have seen a rapid increase in the number of people migrating into Northern Ireland, raising the potential for more pupils to face this form of harassment from fellow pupils. Both the YLT surveys and the DENI survey point to the relationship between general attitudes to minority groups and the propensity to bully people from those groups.

For example, respondents to the YLT 2004–2007 surveys were asked how favourably or unfavourably they felt towards people from a minority ethnic group. Most respondents were very neutral, with around half of respondents in each year saying they felt neither favourable nor unfavourable towards people from a minority ethnic group. However further analysis of the 2005 survey shows a link between how people feel about someone and their actions. Thirteen per cent of those who felt unfavourable or very unfavourable towards people from minority ethnic groups admitted to bullying others, compared to only four per cent of those who felt favourably or very favourable towards such groups (Figure 3.1).

Similarly, in the DENI 2007 survey pupils were asked whether they thought bullying pupils with certain characteristics was wrong or right. Eighty-eight per cent of pupils thought it was always wrong to bully someone because of their

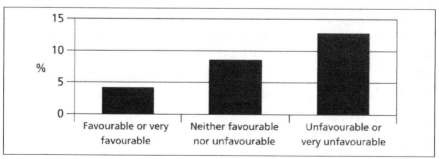

Source: 2005 YLT survey

Figure 3.1 Respondents saying they took part in bullying other students by feelings towards people from minority ethnic backgrounds

race or skin colour compared to 94 and 79 per cent who felt it was always wrong to bully someone because of disability and religion respectively.

How do the rest of the school population respond to incidence of bullying? How do they feel towards the victim of a bully? Are they likely to take action or to remain a bystander?

Findings from the latest Northern Irish research show a strong pro-victim attitude among pupils with over two thirds (64%) saying they feel sorry for someone who is being bullied (Livesey et al., 2007). However it would seem that not everyone with those feelings would translate that into action if they saw someone being bullied. Only 37 per cent said they would try to help the pupil in some way.

This study also showed that the existence of a pro-victim attitude was stronger among girls than boys. While almost three quarters (72%) of girls would feel sorry for someone who was being bullied and wanted to help, this was true for just over half (53%) of the boys. In addition, while 40 per cent of girls said they would definitely not join in bullying of someone they didn't like, this was only true for 24 per cent of the boys. These findings are worrying. They point to a need to address the whole culture within a school, to develop policies and practices that go wider than dealing with specific incidences of bullying, but which seek to build an ethos of tolerance and respect.

This is very much the aim of the National Healthy School Standard (NHSS), which adopts a whole school approach to bringing about and embedding cultural change within a school (NHSP, 2007). The NHSS programme advocates a whole school approach to developing a school ethos that supports learning and promotes the health and well-being of all its pupils and which encourages the participation of everyone within the school community. The NHSS supports schools in achieving a series of standards under four core themes, one of which is emotional health and well-being. One of nine specific standards under this theme relates directly to bullying:

> A healthy school has a clear policy on bullying, which is owned, understood and implemented by the whole school community.

> (DoH, 2005: 9)

Interventions

How do schools respond to the problem of bullying? Research suggests that effective responses will be multi-layered, and require strategies around policy formation and implementation; raising awareness and establishing an anti-bullying culture; and preventing or dealing with incidence of bullying (Smith et al., 2004).

Strategies in each of these areas will become mutually reinforcing. For example, the evaluation of the pack *Focus on Bullying*, prepared for post-primary schools in Northern Ireland, highlights the importance of 'school readiness'; the application of particular initiatives were more successful in schools that had prepared for their introduction and created an ethos that was receptive to such messages (Save the Children, 2005).

The recent study by NCB NI into bullying in primary, post-primary and special schools in Northern Ireland provided further indications that initiatives to address bullying will only be effective if they are delivered within a broad approach to tackling bullying. Among other things this study looked at the help that was available in schools and whether and why pupils used this help.

First of all, it is worth reporting that most pupils do think their school provides real help for people who are bullied. This was true for over half (54%) of respondents to the 2005 YLT survey and to over two-thirds (67%) of post-primary pupils in the NCB NI study. Importantly, however, there is a significant relationship between the perceptions of these pupils about the level of help available in their school and the extent of bullying, as Table 3.1 shows. In both, the NCB NI study and 2005 YLT, pupils who reported that there was 'a lot' of bullying in their school were significantly less likely to think that the school provided real help to pupils who were bullied than respondents who thought that pupils in their schools were bullied 'a little' or 'not at all' bullied.

Table 3.1 Does school provide real help to pupils who are bullied? By extent of bullying in school

| | %| | | | | |
| | YLT 2005 | | | NCB NI study | | |
	A lot	A little	Not at all	A lot	A little	Not at all
Yes	36	54	82	52	71	75
No	49	26	8	33	12	25
Don't know	12	17	9	15	17	0

Sources: 2005 YLT survey and NCB NI study, post-primary school sample.

Moreover, as we shall examine later, pupils are more likely to report lower levels of bullying in schools where they report that: the school has a policy about bullying; that pupils were involved in developing this; that the school has dedicated staff to deal with bullying and that students would talk to that member of staff. These findings once again emphasise the need for positive interaction between policy development, awareness raising activities and creating a positive climate within a school, if specific interventions are to have any impact.

A policy will only be effective if everybody in school has discussed and understood the problem of bullying, and agreed on good and bad practice.

(DfES, 2002: 4)

It is now common for schools to have a particular member of staff whose job it is to deal with bullying. Responses to the NCB NI study suggest this is true for the great majority of schools (79% primary and 77% post-primary) although it is also worth noting that 14 per cent of pupils of all ages did not know whether there was such a member of staff or not, rather negating the value of such an initiative. The respective figures for the 2005 YLT survey were 69 per cent and 17 per cent (Figure 3.2).

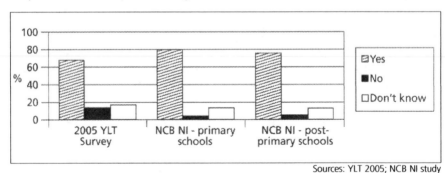

Sources: YLT 2005; NCB NI study

Figure 3.2   Are there particular staff at your school whose job it is to deal with bullying?

Having a dedicated member of staff is only a first step; pupils also need to have confidence that this person can help. The responses of the pupils in the NCB NI study suggest there is still some way to go before this is the case. Among the post-primary pupils, only 15 per cent overall said they would talk to the dedicated member of staff. This figure was almost identical among 2005 YLT respondents.

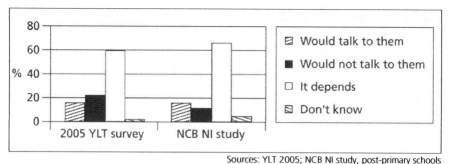

Sources: YLT 2005; NCB NI study, post-primary schools

Figure 3.3   Do you think most people – if they were being bullied – would or would not go and talk to one of these members of staff?

The interactive workshops undertaken during the NCB NI study showed that for many young people talking to a teacher about bullying was simply not a good idea. In the words of one participant, it would 'get the person into trouble so the bully will make it worse'. For most pupils it depended on the circumstances whether or not talking to a teacher was appropriate: 'It depends – it can help but it can also make it worse'. One young person sums up the sort of dilemma many children faced 'If you tell teachers you get bullied more – but if you don't then the bulling continues'.

There was considerable variation (ranging from 4% to 23%) in the responses from pupils from different schools on whether they would talk to the member of staff. This seems to reflect comments from pupils in the discussion groups about the quality of the relationships between staff and pupils and the overall ethos in the school. Students also suggested they are aware of the gap between what a school may say about bullying and what actually happens on the ground: the perspective of the teachers is very often different to that of the pupils, as illustrated here:

We have a system of . . . class prefects. Class prefects can almost certainly work with and approach their class teacher and can make an approach to myself if they feel it is important.

(Vice Principal)

I am a prefect – prefects don't have much of a role – the only thing they are asked to do is set an example.

(Post-primary student)

Development of policies in schools

Despite these question marks about the translation of policy into practice, effective interventions to deal with bullying must start with the development of a school policy to address the issue. The Department of Education in Northern Ireland has made clear its stance on bullying in schools:

Bullying behaviour in whatever form has no place in schools.

(DENI, 2003: 1)

The Education and Libraries (NI) Order 2003 requires all grant-aided schools to include within their discipline policy, measures to prevent all forms of bullying. Further, this Order requires that pupils be consulted on all policies or changes to policies within schools, including those on bullying. This second clause is of particular importance. There is growing evidence of the role played by the school ethos in the effective implementation of school policies on bullying and that a crucial element of a positive school ethos is a school that respects and listens to the views of its pupils. This has been clearly articulated by the Minister for Education in 2001:

A preventative approach to bullying, in its most successful form, takes place within an ethos in which pupils are respected and valued as individuals and where their self-confidence and self-esteem are fostered routinely. A climate of openness, consultation and participation, in which pupil's views are sought, listened to and respected, will do much to build the kind of sound working relationship in which behaviour is no longer an issue and bullying is not tolerated either by staff or by pupils.

(DENI, 2001: 84)

Given these clear policy requirements placed on schools in Northern Ireland it is legitimate to ask some years after they came into effect: to what extent do schools in Northern Ireland have policies on tackling and preventing bullying and are young people involved in developing those policies? These were two of the main research questions raised in the study commissioned by NICCY and addressed by NCB (Schubotz and Sinclair et al., 2006).

With respect to the existence of school policies on bullying, McGuckin and Lewis (2005) surveyed all 1,233 educational institutions in Northern Ireland (910 primary, 167 secondary, 73 grammar, 54 special, 29 further education colleges) on their policies. Unfortunately the response rate was low at 23 per cent, but over 90 per cent of those responding stated that they did have an anti-bullying policy. Most often this was incorporated into the overall pastoral care or disciplinary policy of the school.

All 14 schools in the NCB NI study did have a school policy on bullying. Again, most were incorporated into the overall discipline policy and were seen as part of the pastoral care of the school. It became clear from interviews with principals and staff that there was variation in the extent to which these policies were live documents, used to promote positive cultures and practices in schools and with wide-ranging engagement of staff, parents or children.

The majority of pupils in these 14 schools were aware that the school had a policy on bullying, but not necessarily what that policy said, as the following quote exemplifies:

There is a policy in school on bullying but I don't know much about it – it is not very visible.

(Post-primary student)

The lack of engagement, noted by this student, raises questions about the role and purpose of policies on bullying. From interviews with school managers it seems that some see such documents as being addressed primarily to teachers, with perhaps some consultation with parents. This would seem to reflect long-standing assumptions about the place of students in the school, which has been primarily a passive one. However, interviews also suggested that consideration of the role of pupils in developing bullying policies may begin to test that assumption:

The experience of the students would help [the school] modify the policy.

(Pastoral care teacher)

The perspective of the government in Northern Ireland on involving pupils is clear, as is the Guidance available to teachers:

The creation of an anti-bullying ethos is the result of consultation, careful planning, widespread support and is 'lived' by all.

(DENI, 1999, qf Save the Children, 2002: 24)

It is particularly important that pupils are given the opportunity to contribute to the development of anti-bullying policies.

(DENI, 2001: 85)

Pupil participation in developing policies on bullying

Bullying policies are more likely to be 'live' and to be known and used by pupils if they have been involved in their development. The NCB NI research suggests that this is rarely the case: less than one in three pupils (28%) in post-primary schools had been involved in drawing up the school policy on bullying.

Involving children in the development of anti-bullying policies is only likely to occur where there is a culture of involving children in how their school operates on a day to day basis. The NCB NI study started by asking students about their general involvement in their school. Evidence from the survey shows that only 15 per cent of primary school pupils and under one third of post-primary pupils (32%) said that they were ever asked their views on how something was done in their schools. Only in one post-primary school surveyed did a majority of students (56%) feel that they were asked their views on how something was done in school. The children identified a number of issues where they had a say. Some said they were asked 'if we wanted a library', others 'what is sold in the tuck shop'.

Following on from this, respondents were asked whether they had ever helped to change the way in which things were done in their school. Fewer than one in five primary children (18%) responded positively compared with just over one in ten older children or young people (11%). The sorts of examples the younger children gave reflected the level of participation in the different schools and included:

I help keep the school tidy by picking up the litter.

To put bottles in the canteen and pictures on the walls outside.

I have helped my friend by telling the principal that she is getting bullied.

I was in the school council last year, and we helped bullying, healthier foods in the canteen and more toys in the [play] bins.

Post-primary pupils who felt they had helped change something often referred to work through their schools council:

I am in the school council and we changed the uniform that you could go home in, tracksuit or school uniform.

I am on the school council and we have given ideas on how to improve the anti-bullying process.

I asked for vending machine and they brought in 2 new vending machines with healthy eating options.

Schools councils can be an important mechanism for increasing the involvement of pupils in decision making in school. Two out of five primary schools and three out of four post-primary schools in the NCB NI study sample had a formally established school council. However, the majority of pupils in two out of these five schools did not know that there was a school council or thought that there was not.

There is a school council but it is no good – they don't do anything and no-one knows what they do. They haven't been involved in developing school policy.

(Post-primary student)

This comment by a pupil shows that the mere existence of a school council is unlikely to make much difference unless the council is set up to offer genuine participation and engagement across the whole school population.

Schools councils can offer different levels of pupil involvement or participation. This will reflect the extent to which the school staff genuinely wish to share power with pupils and is often characterised by the role of the teacher within the council. For example: does the teacher chair the meetings, set the agenda and say how things will be done thereby limiting the amount of power offered to students? Or is the council more owned by pupils, so teachers are invited to attend meetings, which are chaired by pupils, to give advice and work together with pupils on the issues the pupils see as important to them? Similarly, the manner in which members of the council are chosen will affect the degree to which all pupils feel some sense of ownership or engagement with the council. Are members of the council selected by staff, are they asked to volunteer, or do all the pupils in the school elect them? Each method reflects different levels of transfer of power to pupils, which in turn is likely to reflect on the effectiveness of the council in engaging with pupils productively (DfES, DH and NCB, 2004).

The wide range of information gathered from the schools in the NCB NI study suggests that the school sample contained examples of schools councils that were ineffective and non-engaging as well as examples of highly participative councils whose activity was part of a wider participatory culture. One school in the study, which had a very active school council, also had a range of other ways of involving the children in the running of the school. This school had developed a range of different mechanisms for dealing with bullying. The principal discussed the range of activities available:

> *The P4 to P7 pupils have a school council and school reps in each class who the children elect themselves. They also have a suggestion box for their ideas. [The pastoral care teacher] looks after the school council. Every class does circle time. Training on circle time is given to teachers on what to do, how to handle it. There's also a bus stop sign where a child stands if they are sad. The other children know that if they see a child standing there that they should go over and ask them to join in with what they're doing. In the school council the children bring up issues to [the pastoral care teacher] and ask for things which may be bought.*

The pupils had participated in a number of anti-bullying programmes and competitions including a quiz that was hosted by an outside agency, an anti-bullying poster competition and a workshop on bullying for children in Years 6 and 7. In addition, both pupils and parents in this school sign an anti-bullying pledge at the start of each new school year. This pledge, along with advice on what to do if bullied, is placed in each child's homework diary so they are constantly reminded of it throughout the school year. While this seems a small thing, there is evidence that if initiatives on bullying are to be effective they need to be constantly revived and repeated (Smith et al., 2004).

This school had an active school council and the councillors were also trained as peer mediators. The pastoral care teacher felt that this gave the children ownership of working through their problems themselves. She commented:

> *They are surprisingly alert. They know a lot more than the teacher does of what's going on. Though in some circumstances you do need the intervention of other members of staff, they can't sort it all out between each other.*

It was also clear from talking to the children that they were very aware of these initiatives – for example, the questionnaire responses show that almost all students (97%) knew about the school council. Further, when asked if there was someone in school they could go to for help if they were unhappy, almost half (44%) of the students at this school mentioned the 'Class Rep' – that is the person representing their class on the school council.

Perhaps it is because of the variation in the operation of the schools councils, noted earlier, that the NCB NI study found some evidence which suggests that schools councils do not have as positive an influence on bullying as other participatory measures. A comparison of the proportions of post-primary pupils who said they thought pupils in their school get bullied 'a lot' according to other characteristics of the school, gives some indications of the sorts of activities within a school which may be helpful in tackling bullying (Table 3.2).

finish 27/02/13

Table 3.2 Proportion of students who thought people in their school were bullied 'a lot', by means of engaging students in tackling bullying

	%		
School has an anti-bullying policy	17	22	School has no anti-bullying policy
Students are involved in developing policy	14	23	Students are not involved in developing policy
School has dedicated staff to deal with bullying	17	30	School has no dedicated staff to deal with bullying
Students would talk to this staff member	7	39	Students would not talk to this staff member
School has a school council	21	18	School has no school council

Source: (Schubotz and Sinclair et al., 2006)

In the summer 2007, NICCY launched new guidance on setting up effective schools councils, which has been sent to all schools in Northern Ireland (NICCY, 2007). As more schools establish schools councils it is important that these operate according to such well-founded guidance on effective practice, especially in the way in which councils can be used to encourage staff and students to work together, as a way of sharing power within the school so as to enhance the level of participation by pupils in decision-making within schools.

The development of schools councils can play a definite role in tackling bullying in schools. The range of perspectives gathered in the NCB NI study suggests that pupils in schools with an active and working school council had a greater sense of ownership of their school. This in turn helps build that positive ethos that is key to establishing a culture that will not tolerate bullying. This relationship is well summarised in a public letter from the Northern Ireland Minister for Education:

It is vital that the school develops a culture in which pupils are confident about expressing their views, and know that their views are listened to, respected and acted upon. Where pupils are used to being consulted about aspects of school life (such as behaviour, school rules, the organisation of the school day, or extra-curricular activities) they will feel more secure individually, about raising particular worries and concerns.

(DENI, 2001: 67)

Culture of pupil participation

Despite this exhortation, the evidence of involvement of pupils in the development of policies on bullying suggests this is not happening (Schubotz and Sinclair et al., 2005). When senior staff were asked about involvement in developing policies, most acknowledged that whilst efforts were made to involve all school staff directly in policy making in schools, pupils were only involved indirectly, if at all. However it was noted that through reflection during the research interviews, many staff revealed a growing awareness that it is good for the general climate of a school to involve pupils in policy making.

The lack of involvement of pupils in the development of policies on bullying strongly reflects a general tendency for schools in Northern Ireland to fail to listen to pupils or involve them in the running of schools. In a major survey of over 1,000 children from 27 different schools across Northern Ireland, children were asked about many aspects of their life and any concerns that they had (Kilkelly et al., 2004; Davey et al., 2005). When asked about school and what they saw as a concern or as unfair in school, although many mentioned bullying, only one in eight (12%) said this was their main concern. For the largest proportion (almost 40%) their greatest single concern was the 'lack of a say' that they had in their school. The respondents listed the many ways in which they were denied a say, and their sense of unfairness that the views of staff were always given precedent over those of pupils. One pupil expressed this as follows:

In school we obviously don't have a say on what happens or what rules are made. But I personally think we should . . . In our school there are grilles on our windows. It makes the school like a prison. A fire could start and we could be trapped and we wouldn't be able to get out the windows. I think this is a disgrace and that something should be done about it. From my point of view, pupils should have a say in what happens in their school.

(Girl aged 14, quoted from Davey et al., 2005: 21)

What is behind this 'lack of a say' or a lack of involvement of pupils in policy development in schools? The interviews with principals and senior staff as part of the NCB NI research suggest this may be due more to the traditional culture of assuming staff know best, than to any strong opposition to involving pupils – especially on a matter such as bullying among pupils where the pupils are much more likely to have pertinent knowledge and awareness. Quite simply, there is not as yet a culture of pupil participation in schools in Northern Ireland. It is not established practice to involve pupils and so many schools had simply not thought about working in this way in developing their policies on bullying. This is despite it being a statutory requirement to do so, the strong messages in the NICCY Guidance available to schools and the growing evidence of the value of working together.

In interviews many respondents attempted to explain their practice of non-involvement of pupils in policy making. The reasons can be grouped under four headings:

- A lack of training or confidence in how to engage positively with pupils in developing policy.
- A lack of time or organisational space to work in this way.
- No sense of shared agenda and hence some suspicion of the motivation of pupils who would get involved.
- A lack of confidence in the competence of pupils to engage productively with staff in policy making.

The studies reported here confirm the clear message given by schools that bullying will not be tolerated. There is also evidence of many schools working hard to introduce a range of initiatives and actions to support that value position. Most pupils also reported that they think their school does provide help to pupils who are bullied, although a substantial proportion do not think this. But research also shows that success in tackling bullying relies on a strong positive ethos in the school and that in turn relies on a school culture that is participatory, where pupils are felt to have a positive contribution to make to the running of their school.

Despite this, with a few notable exceptions, there is little sense that schools in Northern Ireland are at present actively engaging with their pupils to tackle bullying. Involving pupils in the development of school policies is not only a requirement on schools and the right of pupils, it is a core ingredient in the development of effective solutions to reduce levels of bullying in schools. A key message for schools in tackling bullying is the need for them to start to build a culture of participation within their school and to think how best to give pupils a better sense that they are part of the school.

References

ARK. Young Life and Times Survey (1998, 2005, 2006) [computer files]. ARK: www.ark.ac.uk/ylt [Accessed 31 January 2008].

Burns, S. (2006) *School Bullying in Northern Ireland – It Hasn't Gone Away You Know*. Research Update 48. Belfast: ARK. Available at: www.ark.ac.uk/publications/updates/update48.pdf

Childline (2007a) *Facts and Figures. Championing children for 20 years*. Online document. Available at www.childline.org.uk/Factsandfigures2.asp [Accessed 31 January 2008.

Childline (2007b) *Children Calling from Northern Ireland*. Online document. Available online at: http://www.childline.org.uk/content.asp?section = ExtraPage&id = 192 [Accessed 31 January 2008]

Collins, K., McAleavy, G. and Adamson, G. (2004) Bullying in Schools: A Northern Ireland Study. *Educational Research* 46:1, 55–71.

Davey, C. et al. (2005) *An Analysis of Research Conducted with School Children into Children's Rights in Northern Ireland*. NICCY.

DENI (Department of Education, Northern Ireland) (2003) *Department of Education Statement on Bullying*. 17 November 2003. Bangor: DENI.

DENI (2002) *Bullying in Schools: A Northern Ireland Study*. Bangor: DENI, Statistics and Research Branch.

DENI (2001) *Promoting Positive Behaviour*. Bangor: DENI.

Department for Education and Skills (2002) *Bullying: Don't Suffer in Silence. An Anti-bullying Pack for Schools (2nd revised edition)*. London: DfES.

Department for Health, Department for Education and Skills, and National Children's Bureau (2004) *Promoting children and young people's participation through the National Healthy School Standard*. Available online at: www.wiredforhealth.gov.uk/PDF/NHSS_participation_briefing.pdf [Accessed 31 January 2008]

Kilkelly, U. et al. (2005) *Children's Rights in Northern Ireland*. Belfast: NICCY.

Livesey, G. et al. (2007) *The Nature and Extend of Bullying in Schools in the North of Ireland. Research Report*. Bangor: DENI.

McGuckin, C. and Lewis C.A. (2005): *Out of Sight, Out of Mind? Pre-legislative Management of Bully/victim Problems in Northern Ireland Schools.* Unpublished article.

National Healthy Schools Programme (NHSP) (2007) *Whole School Approach to the National Healthy Schools Programme.* London: N80HS-P. Available online at: www.healthyschools.gov.uk [accessed May 2008]

Northern Ireland Anti-Bullying Forum (NIABF): *Strategy 2005–2008.* Belfast: NIABF.

Northern Ireland Commissioner for Children and Young People (NICCY) (2007) *Having your say in Bullying Policies. Guidance to Promote the Involvement of Pupils in Anti-bullying School Policies.* Belfast: NICCY.

Save the Children (2002) *Focus on Bullying: Guidance and Resources for Post-primary Schools.* London: Save the Children.

Save the Children (2005) *Something to Say – Listening to Children.* London: Save the Children.

Schubotz, D. and Sinclair, R. et al. (2006): *Being Part and Parcel of the School. The Views and Experiences of Children and Young People in Relation to the Development of Bullying Policies in Schools.* Belfast: NICCY.

Smith, P. (2005) 'Bullying in Schools'. *Highlight No. 216.* London: NCB.

Smith, P., Pepler, D. and Rigby, K. (Eds.) (2004) *Bullying in Schools: How Successful can Interventions be?* Cambridge: Cambridge University Press.

CHAPTER 4

Honesty about sex and relationships – it's not too much to ask for*

Simon Blake

Introduction

We have made some progress over the past decade or so slowly developing a more positive attitude towards teenage sexuality. But progress is slow. Too many young people are still growing up with shame, guilt and embarrassment about sex. As I travel across the UK visiting Brook services, I hear similar accounts time and again from young people:

We just want someone to talk to.

It was brilliant here at Brook.

They really help you out, listen to you, they treat you right.

Members of my staff confirm that many young people coming to Brook have never really talked to anyone about sex, at home, at school, or anywhere else. As a result they come to services with really 'simple' questions that have been worrying and frightening them. These worries would never manifest with more openness and honesty from a very early age. In 2007, a client at a Brook service asked me:

Why can't they [adults] just be honest . . . sex is fun, isn't it?

I see this as a plea for us adults to sort ourselves out, to lift our heads out of the sand, and start talking honestly about sex, sexuality and relationships with

---

*I am grateful for the significant contribution of Michaela Rafferty to this chapter. Michaela is 21 years old and is a group worker for Brook in Northern Ireland.

46

young people. For me it is an extract from yet another humbling conversation with a young person, which makes me wish we could speed up the process of cultural change.

In this chapter I will address some perennial issues with regard to young people and their sexual attitudes and experiences as well as in relation to Sex and Relationships Education (SRE). I also lay out a youth-led agenda for sexual health for young people – a new agenda that is fit for the 21st century. The chapter is grounded in evidence based on my practice of working in the field of sexual health for many years as well as the Young Life and Times (YLT) survey and sexual health research undertaken elsewhere. It is also illustrated with the views and ideas of Michaela Rafferty, a young woman who has recently started working for Brook in Northern Ireland. I interviewed Michaela and she helped with the development of this chapter by offering her own experience, and reflecting on those of her peers. Her views and perspectives complement the research data I present.

The chapter is divided into six sections. First I will set a general context for this chapter. The three sections following this deal with issues around SRE; experiences of sexual intercourse; and the main influence factors on young people's views on sexual matters. The concluding two sections focus on young people's involvement in setting an agenda for sexual health and on some areas for sexual health advocacy work for young people.

Setting the context – the sexual health of the young

In Britain, the median age of first sexual intercourse is 16 years for both young men and young women (Wellings, 2001). Northern Ireland was excluded from the British NATSAL studies (British National Surveys of Sexual Attitudes and Lifestyles), but the 2001 Northern Ireland Health and Social Wellbeing Survey (NISRA, 2002) found that the average age for first sex was 18 years among males and 19 years among females.

The UK has one of the highest rates of teenage pregnancies in the developed world, second only to the USA and over five times higher than the Netherlands (UNICEF, 2007). Despite a recent downward trend, our teenage pregnancy rates remain stubbornly high. Teenage pregnancy and parenthood is closely related to social exclusion – it is both a cause and consequence. Conception rates are higher amongst those from lower socio-economic groups. On average around one in five pregnancies in Britain end in abortion but in some areas the figure is two in five. Thomson (2000) identified different approaches to sex, with more affluent young people having sex later and investing in the future, whilst those from lower social classes use sexual experience and sexiness to improve social status (ibid). Once pregnant, those from lower socio-economic groups are more likely to continue the pregnancy to birth, whilst young women from areas of greater wealth are more likely to terminate their pregnancy (Social Exclusion Unit, 1999). In Northern Ireland abortion is only available in exceptional circumstances. If women from Northern Ireland want to terminate their pregnancy they therefore have the additional disadvantage that they have to bear the costs of travelling to England, which again may be difficult particularly for young women from poorer backgrounds.

Whilst there is some evidence that condom use is improving and great strides have been made in improving young people's access to condoms, rates of sexually transmitted infections (STI) continue to rise amongst young people in Britain. STI diagnoses and other workload for staff in Genito-Urinary Medicine (GUM) clinics more than doubled in the five years to 2004. More than 750,000 cases of STI's were diagnosed in GUM clinics in 2005. Over one in ten young people screened for Chlamydia test positive. Syphilis diagnoses increased by 23 per cent in 2004/5, compared to the figures for the same period 12 months earlier. According to SOPHID (Survey of Prevalent HIV Infections Diagnosed) from 1996, when effective therapy to treat HIV became available, the number of 16–24 year olds receiving care for HIV in the UK almost trebled and numbers of new HIV infection diagnoses are still expected to rise (HPA, 2006). Whilst more testing and easier access to screening, testing and treatment may have contributed to a rise in reported cases and the uncovering of previously undiagnosed infections, it is also clear that education on STI's and safer sex need to continue. For example, a third of HIV infections in the UK are believed to remain undiagnosed.

It is too easy however to focus on young people's sexual health in medical terms. Underneath the teenage pregnancies and the sexually transmitted infection rates remain poor levels of knowledge about sex, contraception and sexual health. This lack of knowledge often translates into large numbers of young people not making informed choices about their sexual relationships – young people feeling they do not have any choices and who consequently start their sexual career settling for second best and are more likely to suffer from sexual ill health. Gender and other inequalities and prejudice towards, for example, young people who are gay, who are disabled or who come from some minority ethnic community groups contribute to a complex tapestry of sexual health inequalities.

Claims continue to be made that sex education in school and sexual health services for young people promote 'early, easy sex'. The YLT survey shows that this is not the case. YLT found no statistical relation between the frequency of education on sexual intercourse received in school and sexual intercourse experienced by respondents by age 16 (Table 4.1).

Table 4.1 Incidents of respondents' reported sexual intercourse – by lessons, videos or discussions on sexual intercourse received in school

| | % | | |
| | *Lessons received on sexual intercourse* | | |
	No	*Once*	*A few/ many times*
Had no intercourse	78	76	79
Had intercourse once	4	6	4
Had intercourse a few/many times	17	18	17

Source: YLT survey 2004

The 2001 Northern Ireland Health and Social Wellbeing Survey (NISRA, 2002) shows that – if anything – sex education in school is related to a delay in sexual intercourse. NISRA found that only respondents who said that they had received most sex education from their mother were less likely to have had sexual intercourse before they were 17 years of age than respondents who said they received most sex education from school (Figure 4.1). However, as I will show in the next section of this chapter, the quality of sex education delivered in schools still has significant room for improvement.

Sex and relationships education – plugging the gap

The data from the YLT survey shows that less than one in ten respondents (9%) said they either had not had any education or could not remember whether they had any. One quarter (25%) of respondents said they had received

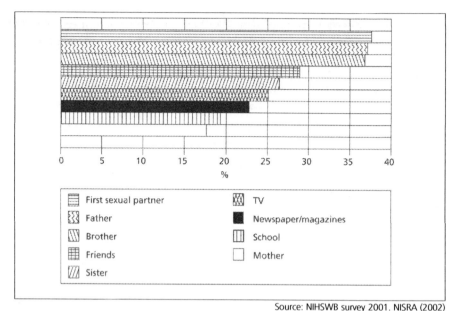

Source: NIHSWB survey 2001. NISRA (2002)

Figure 4.1 Proportion of respondents who had sexual intercourse by age 16, by main source of their sex education (in %)

education on sexual intercourse many times, 45 per cent said a few times and almost one fifth (19%) had classes on intercourse only once. However research and participation work with young people over recent decades has shown that young people – both young men and young women – believe that they receive too little SRE too late and that it is too biological. According to the Sex Education Forum (2000) young people would like more opportunities to explore emotions, relationships and 'real life dilemmas'. The fact that SRE is still not adequate for the majority of young people was also evident in the comments from respondents to the 2004 YLT survey, as the following comments from respondents show:

I feel my school should have been more informative on sex – less biological and more social.

I feel that schools don't teach enough about sex. The reason for this is that they only teach the basic stuff and not any of the side effects of having sex.

In school these issues are not fully addressed. They are taught as a module and many pupils feel the class is only there to fill up the timetable. I do not think they realise how serious the issues are.

In 2006/7 over 27,000 young people responded to a survey about SRE conducted by the UK Youth Parliament. The study entitled *Sex and Relationships Education – Are you Getting it?* (UKYP, 2007) confirmed again that young people do not feel that they are getting the education they need. Forty per cent of 11–18-year old respondents said that their sex education was poor or very poor. Less than half (49%) of respondents knew where their local sexual health clinic was and the majority of respondents had not been taught how to use a condom. Forty-three per cent of all respondents had not been taught about personal relationships in school (ibid).

Michaela's experience supports these findings. Many of her peers got little or no SRE through school, whilst she thinks about herself as 'one of the lucky ones' because she had the opportunity to participate in a sex education project called *Roundabout* run by the Family Planning Association in Northern Ireland:

It was just a relief for someone to finally talk to us about sex. And it was in a friendship group and we got to go on residential visits. The worker made it good, and it was a new face in school, which made it better. At the time I would have been horrified if a teacher had done sex education.

Michaela describes the *Roundabout* project as 'open and practical'. She remembers clearly being able to look at different types of contraception in the contraception kit, which was used as a teaching tool. They also had the chance to practise putting on condoms on a demonstrator. For Michaela all of this was refreshing and interesting because 'they had never spoken about this before'. Previous learning about sex and relationships, including sexual intercourse, had not been particularly reliable because it was always via her peers. The teenage 'rumours and curiosity' meant that she and her peers very often came to their own conclusion about what was true and what wasn't. It is in this context therefore that Michaela felt the advantages of real learning through the participation in the *Roundabout* project. For Michaela, 'being shown that our life is full of choices was definitely one of the most important things' about her experience with Roundabout.

Whilst some (young) people argue that SRE in schools is best taught by outside visitors or indeed other young people there is no evidence that teachers who are trained and supported cannot deliver high quality SRE. As the UK Youth Parliament survey (2007) showed, respondents felt that sex education could be improved immensely if teachers had specific training in the subject area and were able to handle the students' questions (p. 12). What young people really want is someone who feels comfortable talking about sex and someone who can make sure the class is involved, engaged and interested in the lesson.

Brook believes there must be quality support and training for teachers to deliver SRE. At secondary age, we believe like OFSTED (2002) that specialist teams are the most effective way of ensuring effective delivery. Michaela feels that SRE should be treated like any other subject:

I see the importance of it being normalised with young people and being an everyday topic like Maths and English is. And why should you be privileged to get it (SRE) – like I was – and if teachers had the training to do it in a confident and comfortable way, why shouldn't teachers do it?

There is no lack of innovation in SRE teaching practice or resource development. There is certainly excellent practice across the UK, and on a day-to-day basis there are lots of people finding new ways to reach young people with good information and supporting their emotional and social skills. This excellence is evident in creative resources such as *Drunk in Charge of a Body* (Brook, 2005), *Cards for Life* (Blake, 2005) and *Making Sense of Growing Up and Keeping Safe* (Sense Interactive CDs, 2006).

However, the real policy question must be: how do we work with young people to secure equality of SRE provision for all regardless of their gender, sexuality, ethnicity, faith and culture, and also regardless of where and with whom they live, whether they go to school, if they do, which school they go to, and which class they are in when they get to school?

Assumptions are often being made about the quality of SRE in schools with a particular religious ethos. The YLT data show that in Northern Ireland there was no statistical difference between types of school in relation to whether or not 16-year olds had had lessons on sexual intercourse. Overall, approximately nine per cent of students said they had never had such lessons, and this figure was similar in all schools – whether grammar, secondary or planned integrated – and whether they had a predominantly Catholic, Protestant or religiously mixed intake, as Figure 4.2 shows.

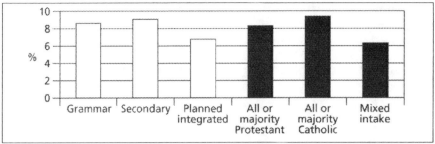

Source: 2004 YLT survey

Figure 4.2 Respondents saying that they had NEVER had lessons, videos or discussion in school on sexual intercourse. By school type

Females were slightly more likely than males to say that they talked about sexual intercourse a few times or many times (73% and 68% respectively), but again statistically, this difference was not significant.

The demand from young people for high quality SRE is widespread (UKYP, 2007). The Sex Education Forum is currently developing materials for schools to help young people 'campaign' for good quality SRE (www.ncb.org.uk/sef).

Michaela's peers also wanted good information about sex and relationships:

> *Other people's reactions [about Michaela being involved in the Roundabout project] were like: What were you doing there? Why were you chosen to do it? It was like it was the secret service – everyone wanted to know about it. What did you learn there? And then when they asked, you passed it on.*

Her belief in clear, accurate information about sex and relationships is linked to what Michaela does now:

> *I knew I wanted to do my work experience at Brook. I gained a passion for it and I knew how important it was for me, that I was ready for the information and I thought, why shouldn't everybody get it?*

Michaela's point about her 'readiness' to receive this information is echoed by Buston and Wight (2002) who emphasise the importance of the timing of SRE in influencing sexual behaviour. According to the authors, there is a need to ensure that SRE is delivered in a timely fashion so that young people have the knowledge, skills and confidence they need to address their 'real life dilemmas as they arise'. It is no good learning about puberty after it has started, sexual attraction when you have felt it, and sexual intercourse when you have had it.

This presents some challenges for teachers and others as there will be young people in any one classroom at different stages of maturity and all their different needs must be addressed. As Michaela said:

I was ready for that information – others may not have been. It may not have immediately had an effect on them so it needs to be made memorable for later.

Experience of sexual intercourse

Research estimates that between one in four and one in three young people in Britain under the age of sixteen are having sex (Erens et al., 2003; Wellings, 2001; NISRA, 2002). This means that a significant majority of the population is not having sex before the legal age of sexual consent (16 years in Britain and 17 years in Northern Ireland). In 2004, YLT found that 78 per cent of 16-year olds had not had sex. This figure was almost identical in the 2007 YLT survey (77%). However, time and again the myth is perpetuated that everyone is having sex under the age of 16 and this becomes part of the perceived social norm.

Perceived social norms are a driving force in youth culture and we must use our understanding of how social norms are developed to provide effective education, which promotes real understanding of the behaviours of others and which in turn enables people to realistically consider their own behaviours (De Silva and Blake, 2006). The pressure to become like everybody else and to conform to a perceived norm puts enormous pressures on young people. Some comments from 2004 YLT respondents are evidence for that pressure to have sex because of the perception that everybody else is doing it:

I presume, many young people uneducated about sexual intercourse, may see it as something everyone is involved in. The media often portrays this.

In the area where I live everyone of my age and even younger, in some cases, do all of these things [drinking, smoking, taking drugs, having sex] and they are all looked upon as normal things to do.

It takes a lot of energy to say 'no', when everyone around you is taking part. At 16 you are considered 'unusual' if you are still a virgin.

Emotional health and wellbeing – how people feel about themselves – is important in determining their decisions about whether and when to have sex. Those who are already more vulnerable may make themselves even more vulnerable through being exploited, hurt or taken advantage of within relationships. We also know there are strong links between sexually risky behaviour and the consumption of alcohol, tobacco and other drugs. The YLT data clearly show this relationship (Table 4.2–4.4).

Table 4.2   Incidents of respondents' sexual intercourse by incidences of consumption of illegal drugs. By survey year

| | % | | | |
| | *YLT 2004* | | *YLT 2007* | |
	Never	*Many times**	*Never*	*Many times**
Never	87	24	86	6*
Once	3	8	3	19*
A few times	6	16	6	38
Many times	4	47	5	38

Source: YLT surveys 2004 and 2007
*Cell counts <5

Table 4.3   Incidents of respondents' sexual intercourse by incidences of consumption of alcohol. By survey year

| | % | | | |
| | *YLT 2004* | | *YLT 2007* | |
	Never	*Many times**	*Never*	*Many times**
Never	100	58	99	53
Once	0	5	0	7
A few times	<1	17	>1	21
Many times	0	18	0	18

Source: YLT surveys 2004 and 2007
*Cell counts <5

In each survey year, only one respondent in the entire sample who had never drunk alcohol had experienced sexual intercourse by age 16, but only 58 per cent of respondents in 2004 and 53 per cent in 2007 who said they had drunk

Table 4.4 Incidents of respondents' sexual intercourse by incidences of consumption of cigarettes. By survey year

| | % | | | |
| | YLT 2004 | | YLT 2007 | |
	Never	Many times*	Never	Many times*
Never	94	41	91	36
Once	2	9	2	8
A few times	2	21	4	26
Many times	2	24	3	30

Source: YLT surveys 2004 and 2007
*Cell counts <5

alcohol many times had never had sex (Table 4.3). Compared with non-drinkers, a higher proportion of non-smokers had had sex, but still less than ten per cent of non-smokers in both survey years had had sex compared with around 60 per cent of respondents who had smoked many times (Table 4.4). In relation to illegal drug use, nearly three quarters of respondents in 2004 (71%) and over nine in ten respondents in 2007 who had taken illegal drugs had also had sexual intercourse at least once (Table 4.2).

From my work at Brook I know that, as the quantity and intensity of alcohol consumption increases, young people visiting our clinics engage in sexual behaviour they may not have engaged in had they not been drinking. Ingham (2002) identified four aspects in which alcohol influences young people's sexual activity:

1. It gives them the confidence to do something they want to do – *anticipated and not unwanted sexual activity.*
2. It allows 'events' to take their course even if they were not planned – *unanticipated and not unwanted sexual activity.*
3. It allows 'events' to take their course but with *unanticipated and unwanted sexual activity.*
4. And finally, alcohol consumption is used to *make sense of behaviours young people would not otherwise have been involved in,* or that they do not perceive to be part of who they are or see themselves as being (e.g., 'I'm not really that type of girl'; 'I don't know what came over me.')

A key challenge for all of us is to ensure that young people know and understand that sexual relationships should be pleasurable, exciting and rewarding. To do this we have to work with young people to help them understand the negative associations between alcohol and sexual activity and empower them to make their own decisions about having sex if and when they are ready rather than feeling pressured to have sex because people around them have. In doing so, we are much more likely to see young people making positive choices about their sexual relationships rather than just passively going along with having sex.

Influence factors on young people's views on sexual matters

The journey through puberty into adolescence and adulthood is one of learning from our own and others' experiences. Michaela puts it like this:

> *A lot of it comes with age – mistakes and close shaves, and experience of others means that you can learn from other people's experiences – those who got caught out, or may have had a scare will learn how not to do it. As you get older you get more confidence in taking responsibility and taking control.*

But is taking responsibility and control more difficult because teenage sexuality is not respected or valued, and sex remains a taboo? Michaela described taboos about young people and sex as a key influence on her attitudes to sexual matters. This is perhaps particularly true in the context of Northern Ireland where monotheistic churches, particularly the Catholic Church and the Protestant churches, have succeeded in maintaining a strong influence on public opinion making and the governance of the majority of schools. Michaela's experience reinforces previous evidence that talking about sex openly and honestly does not always happen, and young people are left with playground gossip, the Internet and friends to piece together and sift for the truths about sex and sexuality.

> *The taboo is still there for young people – talking about it [sex] is not a taboo – will openly boast about it, talking about dangers and the consequences. Also won't talk about pleasure and emotions.*

YLT found that friends were the main influencing factors on respondents' views on sexual matters with family, school and church following behind. There were significant variations with regard to respondents' religious background with church being a much stronger factor for Protestants' views on sexual matters, whilst friends were the most influential factor on the views of those who had no religion (Table 4.5).

Table 4.5 Influence factors on views on sexual matters by religious belonging

	%			
	Religious belonging			
	Catholic	*Protestant*	*No religion*	*All*
My church	11	20	2	13
My family	22	19	25	21
My school	21	15	12	17
My friends	25	28	33	28
Other	6	7	11	7
Don't know	9	7	13	9
Not answered	6	4	3	5

Source: 2004 YLT survey

Agony aunts and other social commentators are also increasingly talking about the impact of the Internet and other media on young people's beliefs and expectations, as some of the quotes from YLT respondents show:

Matters such as these, in my opinion, are glorified by celebs and the media too much, which influences teenagers and sometimes adds pressure.

The changing context and culture is so important in understanding how young people view sex and sexuality. In *All You Need is Love? The Morality of Sexual Relationships through the Eyes of Young People*, Sharpe and Thomson (2005) provide an analysis of young people's sexual morality based largely on the responses of 11–16-year old young people in England and Northern Ireland who took part in a research study on moral values called *The Respect Study*. Sharpe and Thomson outline the changes in sexual norms over a generation:

In the past, there was some certainty (if not total conformity) in relation to the factors which make sex morally legitimate – marriage and procreation. The arrival of accessible contraception opened up a space between sex and procreation . . . The progressive fall in the age of sexual initiation, alongside an increase in the age of marriage and childbearing, suggests that the traditional legitimisation of sex through the institution of marriage and the church is no longer as authoritative as in the past.

(Sharpe and Thomson, 2005: 13)

Most of the young people in *The Respect Study* did think there was a 'right time' for sex and preferably with the 'right person'. They hoped to instinctively recognise the person and the time. One of the statements discussed in the study focus groups was *'You should only have sex if you love someone'*. Young people tended to agree, rather than disagree with this statement. Younger participants, young women and those living in Northern Ireland were more likely to agree with the statement than others involved in the study.

However, findings of the 2005 YLT survey also show that whilst overall a relatively small proportion of respondents (6%) said that they had felt socially pressurised to have sex if they did not want to, this proportion was twice that high (12%) among respondents from not well-off backgrounds, which again emphasises the vulnerability of these young people, as discussed above in relation to unplanned pregnancies.

Michaela highlighted the need for us to recognise the growing gap between the media portrayal of sex and the realities of young lives. She talked about the images of sex in the media – sex as the 'amazing thing' everyone should be experiencing – and how this portrayal has the potential to create a growing gap between expectations and reality, especially since young people continue not to get the information, support and skills to have good relationships:

Self esteem and confidence is so important – many people are having sex instead of love. Some people have their heads screwed on, and they will decide what they want and make sure they are safe. If the message is at home, school and all around you, you can get the message.

Involving youth in the development of sexual health education, services and support

Young people's right to be involved in decisions that affect them is enshrined in Article 12 of the United Nations Convention on the Rights of the Child (1989). One of the examples of young people's policy engagement is Brook's Sexual Health Advocacy Research Project (SHARP) funded by the Camelot Foundation UK. SHARP trains and supports young people to research sexual health issues they are interested in, and then to disseminate their learning to policy makers and practitioners both locally and nationally.

SHARP's most recent survey focused on young people's views on condom advertising. None of the young people taking part in the survey knew that condoms cannot be shown out of their packets on television advertisements, and all of them thought that it is important that the law is changed on this. They produced a short report (Brook, 2007b) and presented their findings to Baroness Joyce Gould, chair of the government's Independent Advisory Group on Sexual Health and HIV at the House of Lords in October 2007. They also talked about their findings in the national and trade press and wrote to the Office of Standards in Communications, the agency responsible for advertising standards. This work has contributed to important national discussions about condom advertising and has formed the basis of Brook's lobbying work in this area.

Brook works within the ethos of the United Nations Convention on the Rights of the Child and delivers clinical services, counselling, education and outreach to over 200,000 young people each year across the UK and the Channel Islands. We are trusted by young people to involve them in all that we do, to put their needs at the heart of everything we do, to maintain their confidentiality, and to lobby and campaign with them and for them. Recently we undertook a youth participation project in Stockton on Tees in England as part of our pledge to improve young people's health (Brook, 2007a). Participants were asked how they wanted schools to involve them in improving SRE and access to sexual health support. They identified ten action points for schools. Some of these were directly related to SRE – for example, arranging for young people to visit sexual health services and communicating about sexual health using new media such as websites, blogs and wikis. However, others were more generally related to the issue of pupil participation; for example the need to listen properly to young people, to establish effective and trustworthy means of communication through school councils, peer educators, school surveys and the provision of confidential space for students where sensitive issues can be discussed. Ruth Sinclair discusses the topic of participation in school in more detail in Chapter 3 of this book.

Towards a conclusion

The politics of sex, sexuality and sexual health have undoubtedly changed in recent times. In the early 1990's the tensions between the moral rhetoric of the conservative right and the pragmatism of emerging public health policy were evident in national policy (Thomson, 1994). This tension was particularly apparent in relation to young people. Too much parliamentary time was spent discussing sexual health policy without regard to young people's stated views and needs. The tiny vociferous minority who opposed sex and relationships education and condemned sexual activity (and the morality) of the young helped journalists to fill column inches without due regard to the facts or the stories behind the statistics.

Over a decade later things have changed, there is no doubt about that. Young people's views are more evident in policy making and practice development. The media for the most part is more balanced and reasoned about sexual morality. The changes that were campaigned for from the 1960s onwards have (at least ostensibly) been achieved – access to contraception, positive guidance on SRE (Department for Education and Employment, 2000; Scottish Executive, 2001 and CCEA, 2001), guidance on confidentiality (Department for Health, 2003), teenage pregnancy and to sexual health strategies across the UK.

But despite this shift there is still not universal equitable provision of SRE as well as confidential sexual health advice and services for young people. And whilst contraception is in principle available to all, in reality many young people feel unable or do not access the help and support they need. Still far too often young people coming to Brook tell us they are not sure whether they had sex because they don't know what it is; or they are having sex which they don't feel in control of, that they are not enjoying and don't want; and they have sex because they thought their friends have had sex, or because they were drunk. In contrast, many of our European neighbours who have more positive attitudes to young people's sexuality report that young people have sex because they thought they were in love. They often realise with hindsight, they were not in love, but this still provides a better context in which to negotiate emotionally and physically healthy sex.

If we do not respond to their request for openness and honesty the consequences for the sexual and emotional health of young people are devastating – devastating to the quality of their relationships and the quality of their sex, and devastating in public health terms evidenced through high teenage pregnancy and STI rates, as well as poor mental health. I therefore want to fast forward to a time where young people grow up:

- Knowing that sex is important, that it can be amazing, life enhancing and fun;
- Understanding that successful relationships are built on trust, mutual respect, openness, hard work, tireless energy, commitment and emotional generosity;
- Supported to develop the emotional and social skills to manage their relationships and sexual health.

Michaela outlines some of the things she would do to improve young people's sexual health:

1. **Trust young people and give them responsibility.** When young people are given choices they will use them wisely. Young people are now being trusted with the word 'sex' in the media (e.g. in music and TV) and in school etc. However, society trusts them with the word, but does not trust them with the support, with services and with the education they need.
2. **Improve services by ensuring they are youth-led.** Services need to have trained staff. Young people have an affinity with other young people. Therefore, adults and young people need to work together encouraging more young people to become professionals in this area. One way of encouraging this is to actively get young people involved in youth and community groups.
3. **Establish more services that young people can get to.** Some sexual health services where advice, contraception, STI and pregnancy testing is available, should be located in school. Services should be more of a full time feature in young people's lives, so they know they can access these when they need to. Currently, patchy services reinforce the message that young people should be ashamed because they are having sex. Often they put their head down when they go through the door, when in fact they are acting responsibly attending these services.

4. **Make Sex and Relationships Education compulsory** in every primary, secondary and special school and pupil referral unit, with a focus on teaching about healthy relationships. Young people must be taught about their bodies and about the other gender as well. This needs to be a regular subject – not just a one-off session and not just for a selected few. It needs to provoke opinions and discussions. Young people need to grow up knowing that it is OK to talk about sex and that we need to talk about sex.
5. **Understand the feelings of a young person.** When a doctor reminds them of their parents it makes them feel uneasy talking about sex. It is really important to focus on having a good relationship with young people so they trust the service provider.

If we really want to bring about demonstrable change and improvement in young people's sexual health and the quality of the relationships and sex they choose, we must recognise that the way we engage with children and young people affects the way they feel, the way they think and their behaviour. We must help young people expect to have good quality relationships, sex that is pleasurable and recognise they have a right and a responsibility to look after their emotional and physical health.

Promoting sexual health is not just about the medical. It is about igniting curiosity, providing new opportunities, new sports and hobbies. It is about establishing pride and embedding self-belief and self-worth. It is about challenging cultures, challenging our own beliefs and assumptions, it is about being honest and open and about working with young people's fears and dreams without being patronising or dismissive. We must be consistent, making sexual health important and reflecting this in the quality of our education, support and services.

At Brook, we believe that young people's trust in our services is underpinned by three essential factors:

1. Remembering to like them, enjoying their humour, their personalities and their 'youthful' fresh perspectives.
2. Believing they are individuals with feelings, aspirations and a developing sense of self. Believing they have promise and talent and are on an important and exciting journey through puberty, into adolescence and adulthood.
3. Remembering what it feels like to be young – the anticipation, the fear, the excitement and the mistakes (and the opportunity these mistakes have for learning) and remaining connected to them and the reality of their lives.

Because we like young people we want the best for them. We want them to have positive relationships, we want them to choose the sex they want and we want them to enjoy and take responsibility for the sex that they have. We are driven to find ways to build relationships through counselling, advice and outreach, promoting self-esteem, raising aspirations, building self-confidence and supporting emotional development. Young people do not want to be punished and they do not want to be made to feel guilty. As Michaela said:

I would like to get the message across that giving information helps young people to make choices and become more responsible for their lives. For me that is the bottom line, being able to make choices – because surely to respect someone you want to help them make choices so they can make choices over their own lives – that is showing respect.

We cannot allow another generation to grow up without that respect, and without positive education about sex and relationships. The emergence of new technologies has brought the potential for information about sexual matters into the bedrooms of young people. Information about sex is available through telephones, computers and digital TV. We cannot be complacent. This information from a range of sources will not always be reliable and it makes it even more urgent that we grasp the nettle and commit to providing the honesty about sex, relationships and sexuality that young people ask for. I, like most sensible adults, see no plausible or desirable alternative.

References

ARK. Young Life and Times Survey (2003–2007) [computer files]. ARK: www.ark.ac.uk/ylt [Accessed 31 January 2008].

Blake, S. (2005) *Cards for Life: Promoting Emotional and Social Development.* London: National Childrens Bureau.

Brook (2005) *Drunk in Charge of a Body II.* London: Brook.

Brook (2007a) *Getting Sex and Relationships Education Right in the North East – Ten Things Young People want Schools to do.* London: Brook.

Brook (2007b) *Condoms Advertising on TV: What Young People Think.* London: Brook.

Buston, K. and Wight, D. (2002) The Salience and Utility of School Sex Education to Young Women. *Sex Education.* 2: 3, 233–50.

CCEA (Northern Ireland Council for the Curriculum, Examinations and Assessment), (2001) *Relationships and Sexuality Education. Guidance for Primary Schools* and *Guidance for Post-Primary Schools*. Belfast: CCEA.

De Silva, S. and Blake, S. (2006) *Positive Guidance on Aspects of Personal, Social and Health Education*. London: National Children's Bureau.

Department for Education and Employment (2000) *Sex and Relationship Education Guidance*. Annesley: DfEE.

Department of Health (2003) *Confidentiality. NHS Code of Practice*. London: DoH.

Erens, B. et al. (2003) *National Survey of Sexual Attitudes and Lifestyles II: Reference Tables and Summary Report*. London: National Centre for Social Research.

HPA (Health Protection Agency) (2006) *HIV and other Sexually Transmitted Infections in the UK. 2006: Chapter 5.4. Young People*. London: HPA. Available online at: www.hpa.org.uk/publications/2006/hiv_sti_2006/pdf/Part%205/part5_young_people.pdf [Accessed 31. January 2008]

Ingham, R. (2002) *Young People, Sex and Alcohol*. London: Sex Education Matters.

National Children's Bureau (2004) *It's More than just Listening: Children and Young People talk about Participation*. London: NCB.

NISRA (Northern Ireland Statistics and Research Agency) (2001) *Northern Ireland Health and Social Wellbeing Survey*: NISRA.

OFSTED (Office for Standards in Education) (2002) *Sex and Relationships*. London: OFSTED.

Scottish Executive (2001): *Sex Education in Scottish Schools. Summary of National Advice*. Learning and Teaching Scotland: Dundee.

Sense Interactive CDs (2006) *Making Sense of Growing Up and Keeping Safe* Kent: Sense Interactive CDs.

Sex Education Forum (2000) *Young People's Charter for Good Sex and Relationships Education*. London: NCB.

Sharpe, S. and Thomson, R. (2005) *All you Need is Love? Sexual Morality through the Eyes of Young People* London: NCB.

Social Exclusion Unit (1999) *Teenage Pregnancy*. London: HMSO.

Thomson, R. (1994) Moral Rhetoric and Public Health Pragmatism: The Recent Politics of Sex Education. *Feminist Review*. 48.

Thomson, R. (2000) Dream On: The Logic of Sexual Practice. *Journal of Youth Studies* 3: 4, 407–27.

United Nations Convention on the Rights of the Child 1989. Available online at: www.unhchr.ch/html/menu3/b/k2crc.htm [accessed 31 January 2007]

UNICEF (2007) *Child Poverty in Perspective: An Overview of Child Well-being in Rich Countries. A Comprehensive Assessment of the Lives and Well-being of Children and Adolescents in the Economically Advanced Nations. Report Card 7*. Innocenti Research Centre: UNICEF.

UKYP (2007) *Sex and Relationships Education – Are you Getting it?* United Kingdom Youth Parliament.

Wellings, K. et al. (2001) Sexual Behaviour in Britain: Early Heterosexual Experience. *The Lancet*, 358: 9296, 1843–50.

CHAPTER 5

Diversity or division? Experiences of education in Northern Ireland

Tony Gallagher

Northern Ireland is a small place. Despite this it has a plethora of schools and an even greater plethora of school types. There are many reasons for this, but most of them gravitate around the historical role of the churches in education in Ireland, up to the 1920s, and in Northern Ireland since partition. The National School system was established in 1833 and although the Dublin Administration aspired towards a common school system for children of all denominations, within a relatively short period the main churches on the island had all asserted control over 'their' schools and the system was denominational in all but name (Akenson, 1970).

After partition in 1921/2 the new Northern Ireland government embarked on a plan to reduce the role of the churches in education in favour of new local authorities. In some respects they wished to break from the legacies of the National School system and swing in behind the pattern of educational development that had emerged in England and Wales from the latter part of the 19th century onwards (Akenson, 1973). Once again the official ambition was that, at best, a common school system might develop over time. More realistically, but still somewhat ambitiously, the inaugural Minister of Education hoped that the main churches, including the Catholic Church, would develop a relationship with the local authorities and, through them, with the new Northern Ireland government.

Once again the ambition would remain unfulfilled. Not only did the Catholic Church eschew any relationship with local authorities, preferring instead to maintain a stout, if impecunious, independence, but the main Protestant Churches also refused to hand their schools over to local authority control. Refused, that is, until they won significant concessions from the Northern

. that rendered the new state schools as Protestant in all but ...e 'integrity' of the denominational divide in schools became ...ed, not to be challenged until the 1980s when the first planned . school opened. By 2008 the integrated sector had undoubtedly ...ned its place, but the proportion of children attending integrated sc... ...ols still sat at about seven per cent and there were precious few instances of schools with 'mixed' enrolments throughout the rest of the education system. Denomination, then, rests as one of the key characteristics of the schools system in Northern Ireland and is one of the reasons for the promiscuous nomenclature of school types. But it is not the only reason.

Virtually alone outside the German-speaking states of West/Central Europe, Northern Ireland is one of the few places that still operates a system of academic differentiation into separate school types at the end of primary education. Free secondary education was established by the 1947 Education Act. In common with most parts of the United Kingdom the system adopted involved separate grammar and secondary schools, with the use of transfer tests to determine who would be offered the coveted places in the grammar schools. Unlike the rest of the United Kingdom, Northern Ireland retained academic selection and separate post-primary schools in the face of evidence on the social unfairness and educational inequities such a system produces (for the most recent evidence see Gallagher and Smith, 2000). As we will see below, this issue is much debated and even managed to secure a key place on the agenda of the peace talks. But for the present, the main significance is that a system of separate post-primary schools adds further to the institutional mix of school types, not least because there developed parallel systems for Protestants and Catholics.

As will already be appreciated, education in Northern Ireland is nothing if not nostalgic, and many privilege the stolid authority of past practice and tradition as lodestones of organisation. A further consequence of this is that Northern Ireland probably has a disproportionate extent of single-sex schools in comparison with most other modern education systems. Traditionally this may have largely been a consequence of Ultramontane Catholicism and its fixation with maintaining the separation of the sexes. And it is true that, in recent years, there has been a general movement towards co-educational schooling, but there still remain many single-sex schools amongst the socially elite grammar sector.

This, then, is the context for schooling that would confront the ubiquitous 'visitor from Mars' who cast their vision upon the education system in Northern

Ireland. It has been said that it is a system which divides pupils in every way imaginable. Certainly, as we have seen, it is a system which has institutionalised denominational, ability and social differences and, to a significant extent, gender differences. Whether the institutionalisation of these differences leads to a creative pluralism or an enervating conservatism is a subject of much debate. In this chapter we will examine what light some of the evidence from the Young Life and Times (YLT) survey may throw on these issues.

Chapter 1 in this collection, written by Duncan Morrow, examines the survey evidence on community relations, so it would be idle to repeat that focus here. Suffice to say that recent patterns have been fairly consistent in that most of our respondents say they have had contact across the sectarian divide and most have participated in cross-community events. Despite this, most also think that religion will always be important in Northern Ireland. Catholic respondents are somewhat more optimistic than Protestants on the prospects for improved community relations, but Catholics are also more likely to say that they would choose 'own-religion' schools for their children. In 2004 we asked our respondents which among a series of influences had the most important effect on their views of the other main religious community. Overwhelmingly and consistently the most important influence was the family (46%), followed by friends (16%), Church (10%) and only then schools (8%). Interestingly, in view of personal choice for school types noted above, a higher proportion of Catholics identified the school as an influence, in comparison with Protestants (10% versus 5%), but even for Catholics it was still ranked fourth in ascribed significance. Assuming this self-perception is accurate then it could lead to one of two conclusions: first, that schools exert such little influence in comparison to the other sources that community relations work is possibly misguided and probably not cost-effective; alternatively, of course, the result may simply highlight the challenge facing educators in attempting to tackle these issues, for if they do not accept that challenge, then who will?

Dividing children at eleven – attitudes to academic selection

The debate over the future of academic selection at age 11 years has been one of the most intense debates in education in Northern Ireland over the past decade. The basic timeline of the debate begins with the arrival of the New

Labour government in 1997 and the decision of the minister with responsibility for education to commission research evidence to inform debate and discussion. Two research studies followed, one focusing on the system of delayed selection at age 14 years operated in the Craigavon area (Alexander et al., 1998) the other focusing more widely on the consequences of academic selection at age 11 years (Gallagher and Smith, 2000). Following the publication of these research reports, a Post Primary Review Body was established to consult on the issues and bring forward recommendations. The Review Body's report recommended an end to academic selection at 11 years, the implementation of a new system of formative assessment through primary school and the coordination of post-primary schools into a series of collaborative collegiates (Burns Report, 2001). There followed another period of consultation on these recommendations and a report on the results of this process, followed by the establishment of a Post Primary Review Working Group comprised of educational interests. The report from this group (The Costello Report, 2004) also recommended the end of academic selection at age 11 years, the use of formative assessment, but rather than endorse the idea of collaborative collegiates, this report recommended an 'entitlement curriculum'. This would require all schools to provide a choice of a set minimum number of subjects for pupils at the ages of 14–16 years, and 16–18 years, with at least one third of the options being broadly academic and at least one third broadly vocational. The intention was that all pupils would have access to the same broad range of curriculum options so that appropriate and suitable pathways could be chosen. It was recognised that the implementation of the entitlement curriculum would probably require schools to engage collaboratively with other schools.

There followed another period of discussion before most of the measures outlined above were incorporated into the 2006 Education Order. This Order also implemented the Revised Northern Ireland Curriculum, which included the provisions for the entitlement curriculum. At almost the last minute an intervention arose from the political talks underway to re-establish the Northern Ireland Assembly. This intervention meant that the ban on academic selection at age 11 was made dependent on a formal endorsement by the Northern Ireland Assembly. This position was reconfirmed in the 2007 St Andrews talks, after which the Northern Ireland Assembly was reconvened and a new power-sharing arrangement established between the four main political parties, with the DUP and Sinn Féin as the predominant partners. Copies of the research and related materials can be found at: www.deni.gov.uk/index/22-postprimaryarrangements-new-arrangements_pg/resources. htm [last accessed 1 February, 2008].

The public debate on this issue has, not surprisingly, been dominated by adult voices. The Gallagher and Smith (2000) research did include focus groups with school pupils, while a parallel study (Leonard and Davey, 2001) collected data specifically from primary school children. A number of groups of pupils and young people made submissions to the Post Primary Review Body, while the consultation on the Body's recommendations included focus groups of young people coordinated by the Youth Forum. That said, the pattern of views among young people largely mirrored those of the adult community. Thus, for example, Gallagher and Smith (2000) had concluded that the system of academic selection at 11 years was divisive not only among schools and teachers, but also among pupils, parents and the wider public. In essence they argued that people who were going through, or who had gone through, the grammar school route tended to be largely supportive of the current arrangements, while those who had gone through secondary schools tended to be more critical. This pattern had emerged specifically from the Northern Ireland Life and Times (NILT) survey of adult respondents (see also Gallagher and Smith, 2001).

In this chapter, we examine evidence from previous YLT surveys to see if the same patterns emerged. The survey in which these issues were most directly examined was carried out in 1999, which included all 12–17-year-olds living in the same household as a respondent to the NILT survey. The basic pattern of results found across the sample are shown in Table 5.1.

Overall, then, the pattern of results suggests that most of the sample think that the 11-plus puts too much pressure on children and that it happens at too young an age. On the other hand, most also feel that selection has to happen at some point in a child's education and that non-grammar (secondary) schools provide an excellent education. Only a bare majority feel that the 11-plus system makes most children feel like failures. On the other three items only a third, or slightly more than a third, of the sample agree; thus, most do not agree that the system of separate grammar and secondary schools is unfair, or that grammar schools provide the best education in the UK. However, a little less than a third agree that the 11-plus provides a good test of ability.

As noted above, however, past survey evidence has suggested a difference in opinion depending on one's personal experience of the system and the same

Table 5.1   Agreement with the statements relating to the 11-plus test

	%
The 11-plus puts too much pressure on 10 and 11 year olds	72
Selection has to happen at some time in a child's education	71
Children who don't get places at grammar schools still get a first class education	65
Children are too young at age 10 or 11 for selection tests	63
The 11-plus system means that most children feel like failures	50
A system of separate secondary and grammar schools is unfair	37
Grammar schools provide the best standard of education in the UK	32
The 11-plus is a good measure of ability	31

Source: 1999 YLT survey

was true for our sample in 1999. Thus, while there was overall agreement on the first three items in Table 5.1 among pupils in grammar and secondary schools, there were marked differences between them in the certainty of opinion. For example, while almost three quarters overall felt that the 11-plus puts to much pressure on 10- or 11-year-olds, this was so for 80 per cent of secondary pupils, but only for 60 per cent of grammar pupils. On the other two of these items the difference between the groups was mainly reflected in the strength of opinion: whereas 17 per cent of grammar pupils strongly agreed that selection was inevitable at some point in a child's education, this was so for only 6 per cent of secondary pupils. In the same vein, whereas 12 per cent of grammar pupils strongly agreed that non-grammar schools provided a first class education, this was so for 30 per cent of pupils from secondary schools.

Of the remaining items, opinion was significantly different among grammar and secondary pupils on three statements. Thus, whereas 53 per cent of grammar pupils agreed that grammar schools provided the best education in the UK, this was so only for 20 per cent of pupils from secondary schools. Almost three quarters of secondary pupils felt that children aged 10 or 11 years were too young for academic selection and 58 per cent said that the 11-plus makes most children feel like failures; by contrast, these views were held by 47 per cent and 37 per cent of grammar school pupils respectively.

On the remaining two items the balance of opinion was not in agreement with the statement, but there were again marked differences in the views of grammar and secondary pupils. Thus, whereas 47 per cent of grammar pupils felt that the 11-plus was a good measure of ability, this was so for only 21 per cent of pupils from secondary schools. And while 45 per cent of pupils from secondary schools felt that the system of separate grammar and secondary schools was unfair, this was so for only 25 per cent of pupils from grammar schools.

Another issue where we found a significant difference between grammar and secondary pupils in our 1999 survey lay in their views on what should happen next. In particular, whereas only a minority of grammar pupils (36%) felt that the system of academic selection at age 11 years should be changed, this was so for a majority of secondary school pupils (51%). There also were interesting differences in the preferred type of change. Hardly any of those who advocated change felt that all that needed to be changed was the system of grammar and secondary schools, that is, with the 11-plus left intact. However, among the minority of grammar pupils who advocated change, many more felt that only the 11-plus tests needed to changed, in comparison with secondary pupils (59% versus 29%). By contrast, many more of the secondary pupils, in comparison with grammar pupils, felt that the 11-plus tests and the system of separate schools needed to be changed (44% versus 28%).

This difference was highlighted also when we asked the respondents who favoured some kind of change in the system about various possible options for change. The proportions who felt that a specific suggestion for change was fairly or very useful are shown in Table 5.2.*

We can see from the table that views range widely, from a third who say that selection should occur at age 16 years, to two thirds who say selection should occur at age 14 years. A significant proportion also suggest that the mechanism of selection at age 11 should change (to teacher assessment, or the same test taken at a later time in the school year, or a different type of test altogether). For these items there were fewer instances of distinct differences between grammar and secondary pupils, although it should be kept

---

* These questions were not asked of the all respondents – some were asked of those who thought the 11+ should be changed, whilst others were asked of those who thought the secondary/grammar system should be changed.

Table 5.2 Agreement with statements on selection

	%
Have some kind of selection test later at age 14	67
Instead of a test, have the children assessed by their teachers	59
All children go to the same school until age 17 and then split to do either 'A' levels or for vocational training	51
Have the test at the end of the Primary 7 year instead of the beginning	46
All children go to the same school until age 14 and then split to either secondary or grammar schools	45
Have a different kind of test	38
Allow any secondary school that wishes to select up to a third of their pupils for a 'grammar' stream	36
Have some kind of selection test later at age 16	35

Source: 1999 YLT survey

in mind that here we are dealing only with the views of the minority of grammar pupils who felt the system did require some sort of change. Interestingly, for these grammar pupils the preferred alternative tended to be later selection at age 14 years.

Interestingly, but perhaps not surprisingly, there were some differences between the views of those who passed, failed or did not take the 11-plus tests. As might be expected, the broad pattern on most items was that those who 'passed' the 11-plus tended to be more favourably inclined towards the selective system, while those who 'failed' or did not take the tests tended to be more critical. However, there were occasions when the views of the latter two groups divided. Thus, for example, those who did not take the 11-plus tests were stronger in their view that the 11-plus tests put too much pressure on children and that age ten or eleven years was too young an age to take these tests. By contrast, those who failed the 11-plus tests were stronger in their view that the system of separate secondary and grammar schools was unfair, and that the 11-plus means that most children feel like failures.

In our 2003 survey of 16-year olds we asked a small number of these questions again and received largely comparable answers and pattern, despite the different sampling methodology and age group. Thus, while a majority still agreed that the 11-plus places too much pressure on 10- and 11-year-olds, secondary school pupils were significantly more likely to agree strongly with this proposition. Similarly, while a clear majority in 2003 felt that selection had to happen at some point in a child's education, grammar pupils were significantly more likely to agree strongly with this view.

At the time of writing the debate on the future of post-primary education remains as strong, and unclear, as at any point over the past number of years. Throughout this period, and throughout the debate there has been a marked pattern such that those who benefit from the current arrangements have raised their voices loudest in defence of the status quo, or of limited change, whereas those who benefit least from the current arrangements have tended to favour more drastic amelioration. Our examination of YLT survey data for 1999 and 2003 suggest that on this issue at least, the youth of Northern Ireland are remarkably similar in their views to their parents.

Gender and aspirations for education and employment

As the final drafts of the present text were being prepared the Department of Education issued a consultation paper on a new school improvement policy entitled *Every School a Good School* (Department of Education, 2008). Amid a welter of statistics and analysis a pattern which stood out, if only for its ubiquity, was the performance gap between boys and girls, to the advantage of the latter. This pattern is not new, of course, having been evident in average patterns for GCSE for many years, and it is certainly not unique to Northern Ireland. Less obvious, however, is an accurate diagnosis of why this pattern should remain so persistent and, in consequence, the identification of ameliorative measures. The results of the YLT survey cannot, unfortunately, plug this policy and practice gap, but it does contain some evidence which might be of interest to those seeking an answer to this most intractable of questions. Over a series of surveys we asked our respondents to indicate where they thought they would be in at the beginning of the next school year and at the same point in two years time. Table 5.3 provides some of the answers provided by our sample to the first of these questions:

Table 5.3 Activity in following October

By next October I will be . . .		2003	2004	2005	2006
				%	
. . . in full-time school or college	Male	55	60	57	52
	Female	58	65	58	61
. . . in full-time work	Male	7	6	3	7
	Female	3	1	2	1
. . . in part-time college and part-time work	Male	21	18	26	21
	Female	32	25	31	30
. . . on a training scheme	Male	14	11	12	18
	Female	4	5	6	5

Sources: 2003–2006 YLT surveys

As we can see clearly from the table, the majority of our respondents expect still to be in full-time education at the beginning of the next school year, while the next most popular prediction is that they will be attending college on a part-time basis and undertaking part-time employment. However, there are interesting gender differences in aspiration, even at this early stage of prediction. We can see from the table that a slightly larger proportion of girls plan to be in full-time education, but the difference in terms of educational engagement is most marked for those expecting to be in part-time college/employment, where the proportion for female respondents is markedly higher in comparison to male respondents. By contrast, significantly more males expect to be on a training scheme or even in full-time employment.

These gendered patterns of aspiration toward education and employment become even more marked when we look at the responses to the question on where they expected to be in October two years hence – see Table 5.4.

For this question the modal response remains the prediction to be in full-time education, but the gender difference in aspirations beyond this have widened: for young women the second most predicted outcome is to be in part-time education and part-time employment, while for young men it is generally to be in full-time employment. It is also noteworthy that the proportion of young

Table 5.4 Activity in next two years

By October two years from now I will be . . .		%			
		2003	*2004*	*2005*	*2006*
. . . in full-time school or college	Male	43	45	40	39
	Female	44	53	43	49
. . . in full-time work	Male	28	23	19	25
	Female	16	12	12	11
. . . in part-time college and part-time work	Male	17	19	28	23
	Female	34	27	37	33
. . . on a training scheme	Male	7	8	8	11
	Female	2	3	4	3

Sources: 2003–2006 YLT surveys

men who predict they will be on a training scheme remains markedly higher than that of young women.

We can only speculate here on the full implications of this gendered pattern of responses. The greater orientation of males towards employment and females towards education may reflect comparative confidence on the ease of gaining employment: young men may be more likely to perceive that there are worthwhile job opportunities available, whereas more young women may feel that adequate employment may be more likely with greater credentials. On the other hand, it is possible that the patterns reflect greater alienation among young men towards education and a greater desire to get out and start earning money.

There was an attempt to throw some additional light on these issues in these surveys. In 2003 and 2004 we asked a series of questions about attitudes to school. In 2005 we asked more specifically about perceived links between employment and education. And in 2006 we asked some additional questions on attitudes to school experience. Although none of these provide a definitive explanation for gendered differences in aspiration, they do provide some indications of possible lines of speculation.

In 2003 and 2004 we asked a series of questions on attitudes to school: in 2003 we asked for simple yes/no responses, but in subsequent years we asked for levels of agreement or disagreement. Keeping those operational differences in mind, the pattern of results is presented in Table 5.5.

Table 5.5 Attitudes to school*

| | 2003 | | 2004 | |
| | % saying yes | | % agreeing or strongly agreeing | |
	Male	Female	Male	Female
School provided me with skills and knowledge for later life	69	80	70	80
Some teachers really inspired me	58	68	59	73
School opened my mind	50	64	43	60
I was bored at school	33	24	27	15
School didn't teach me to think for myself	28	21	23	17
School was almost all listening and no doing	27	24	23	15
I did not enjoy learning at school	25	17	20	11

Source: 2003 and 2004 YLT surveys
*Note: in 2003 the figure is for the % saying yes; in 2004 the figure is for the % saying agree or strongly agree

The overall pattern represented by these responses is, of course, very positive: most young people say that school provided them with the skills and knowledge that they would need for later life, that some teachers inspired them and that school helped to open their minds. At the same time, only a minority say they were bored at school, or that school did not teach them to think for themselves, or that school was all listening and no doing. And the lowest proportion of all said that they did not enjoy learning at school. However, alongside this general positive picture, we can also see that female respondents are almost always more positive on the positive items, while male respondents are more negative on the negative items. Within the context of an overall positive environment, in other words, our evidence here points to a slightly lower level of positive engagement among young men.

In 2006 we asked slightly different questions on related themes and found broadly the same pattern of results (see Table 5.6). That is, overall most respondents were very positive about their experience of school, but there was

Table 5.6 Respondents agreeing with the statements on school experience

	%	
	Male	*Female*
At school I was allowed to express my views	65	72
I was happy at school	63	77
I am satisfied I achieved to my full ability	61	72
Most teachers did not respect me as an individual	21	13

Source: 2006 YLT survey

a difference in extent between males and females suggesting that the former were somewhat less engaged in the educational process.

In 2005, by contrast, we asked a series of items which were much more specifically geared towards perceptions of the link between education and employment. This was also the time at which the Education Maintenance Allowance (EMA) was being introduced to attempt to encourage more young people to stay in education beyond the compulsory age. Perhaps unsurprisingly, 89 per cent of our respondents had heard of the EMA. About two-thirds of them said they had heard about the EMA at school, a proportion far higher than any other potential source of information. When we asked whether the EMA had influenced their decision about staying in school beyond the compulsory age, only three per cent said it had affected their decision a lot, but a quarter said it had affected their decision a little. There was, however, an interesting gender difference when we asked if their decision would have been affected if they had known about the EMA: in this case only eight per cent of male respondents said it would have affected their decision, but this view was expressed by 24 per cent of female respondents.

We then asked a series of more general questions on the link between education and employment, with the following pattern of results:

A majority of respondents clearly recognise the value of education and most are censorious towards a dependency lifestyle. However, for these items perhaps the main point of note is the limited difference between male and female respondents, certainly in comparison to the items considered above.

So where does this leave us? The evidence of our surveys suggests that young men's aspirations are somewhat more oriented than young women's towards seeking employment, whereas young women's aspirations

Table 5.7 Respondents agreeing with statements on attitudes towards education

	%	
	Male	*Female*
Staying in full time education improves your career prospects	83	91
Staying in full time education leads to higher salaries	50	52
There is nothing wrong in relying on benefits after leaving school	17	14

Source: 2005 YLT survey

are somewhat more oriented towards education (see Table 5.7). All recognise the correlation between educational experience and employment prospects, so the different aspirations do not appear to be driven by different perceptions of the value of education. It may be that males are more confident about the prospects of gaining employment than females, although whether this confidence is realistic or not may be open to question. Alternatively it may be that young men seek more short-term goals, whereas young women are more ambitious in the longer-term. The third possibility, and perhaps the one most closely linked to the wider pattern of data presented here, is that a slightly higher proportion of males than females have a somewhat more negative experience of schooling. If true, this might suggest that the 'employment orientation' of males is less to do with the attraction of employment and more to do with the dissatisfaction with school.

Citizens of the future

The table above shows us that over two in three males and almost three in four females said that they were able to express their views in school. For some reformers of the education system in Northern Ireland this will be a heartening result. As we saw at the start of this chapter, our respondents generally feel that school has a limited influence on their perceptions of the other main religious community. Despite this, education has been seen as one of the key vehicles for promoting better community relations, either through curriculum initiatives, contact programmes to bring young Protestants and Catholics together, or through integrated schools (Gallagher, 2004). Perhaps the most straightforward way to address this is through the curriculum and the evidence of our surveys is that, generally, young people are supportive of this.

In 1999, for example, we asked 12 to 17-year olds whether they agreed or not whether schools should teach a number of different issues. Most felt that Catholic schools should offer sports such as cricket or rugby (72%) and that Protestant schools should offer Gaelic sports (71%). In the same vein, most agreed that schools should teach about all religious festivals (62%) and all religious beliefs (62%), and over two-in-five (43%) said that schools should teach about Protestant religious beliefs. However, only a small minority (10%) felt that schools should teach Ulster-Scots culture and language. Most also disagreed that religion is something that should be left to parents and churches and not be included in school. On most of these items the Catholic respondents tended to be more supportive than Protestant respondents. There were also some issues on which the view of Catholic respondents were more markedly favourable: thus, for example, 52 per cent of Catholics, but only six per cent of Protestants, said that schools should teach Irish culture and language, and while 65 per cent of Catholics said that all schools should teach Catholic religious beliefs, this was so for only 27 per cent of Protestants. Inter alia, in 1998 we asked for our respondents' views on evolution and while 78 per cent of Catholics agreed that human beings developed from earlier species of animals, this was so for only 49 per cent of Protestants.

The general judgement on curricular and other interventions in education over the years is that it has been limited (Gallagher, 2004). For this reason the recently established (2006) Revised Northern Ireland Curriculum has included a new citizenship programme to address issues related to rights, equality, justice and democracy (Smith, 2003; Lundy and McEvoy, 2007; McEvoy, 2007). Obviously the development of a citizenship education programme in a society emerging from a quarter century of political violence offers particular challenges to educators, although in our 1998 survey we found that 60 per cent of our respondents said that citizenship education definitely or probably should be included in the school curriculum, with the level of support being a little higher among grammar school pupils.

In our 1998 and 2006 surveys we tentatively broached this issue by asking about the operation of school councils. It should be emphasised that the citizenship curriculum is about much more than school councils, but an effective and influential council may mark a participatory approach to school governance that is moving in the direction advocated by the Convention on

81

the Rights of the Child in the recognition of pupil voice (Lundy, 2007). The starting point is that the proportion of respondents who say that their school had a school council involving pupils and teachers has gone up from 42 per cent in 1998 to 57 per cent in 2006. On the other hand, in 2006 53 per cent said that their school council was not very effective in raising and influencing issues affecting school life. Furthermore, we did ask them to identify which among a range of issues they felt were influenced by school council and found little change over the two survey periods (see Table 5.8).

Table 5.8   Influence of School Councils

Percentage saying that their School Council is able to influence school policy on . . .	%	
	1998	2006
. . . school facilities	46	43
. . . school policies	Not asked	43
. . . school uniform	20	23
. . . the curriculum	11	10
. . . budget allocations	Not asked	7

Source YLT surveys 1998 and 2006

One area where significant change arose was when we asked if there were any other areas which the council influenced: in 1998 only ten per cent said that there were other areas, but by 2006 this had risen to 27 per cent. For our 2006 respondents, the most frequently mentioned area of influence was school meals (46%), followed by a fifth each who said that their school council had some influence on the issues of school formals and events, and charity and fund-raising activities.

In our 1998 survey we had also asked about long-term plans and found that as many as 44 per cent of our respondents said they were likely to leave Northern Ireland. The most important reason for leaving (58%) was to attend college or university, especially among grammar school pupils. Thereafter 48 per cent said they would leave to seek a better future and 44 per cent said they would leave because there were better job prospects elsewhere. Only ten per cent said they would leave because of the 'Troubles' and only six per cent said the decision was influenced by other factors. Interestingly there were no differences on these items between respondents who were Protestant, Catholic or who said they had no religion.

Conclusions

This chapter began by highlighting the institutional pluralism of the schools system in Northern Ireland and asked whether this had positive or negative effects. We have examined some evidence from the YLT survey on the experience and views of Protestants and Catholics, males and females, and young people from grammar and secondary schools. Perhaps unsurprisingly the pattern varies across the social dimensions. On many of the issues we have examined, bar specific examples, Protestant and Catholic young people hold many views in common and are reasonably well-disposed towards recent initiatives through education to address various aspects of community relations. Catholics tend, in general, to be a little more positively inclined towards most initiatives and a little more optimistic for the future, but the most striking emergent picture from the body of evidence is commonality of perspective.

So too, in many respects, when it comes to gender. Most young people in Northern Ireland are well disposed towards school and education, and have generally positive attitudes towards their teachers. That said, there does appear to be a minority of pupils who express a degree of alienation from schools and this minority appears to include a disproportionate number of young men. There is some evidence, for example, to suggest that males are a little more likely than females to focus on gaining employment, whereas female respondents appear to be more focused than male respondents on options for post-compulsory education. It is unclear whether this is due to misplaced confidence among young men on the promise of the labour market, or a more (mature?) long-term focus on the part of young women. The evidence here suggests the possibility that the attraction of the labour market to boys is perhaps reinforced, to some degree, by an element of alienation among young men. Further diagnosis of this issue is important as there is a persistent performance gap to the disadvantage of young men.

The third and final issue of note lies in views on the future of post-primary education and, more particularly, the system of academic selection at the end of primary school. This is an issue that has been hotly contested for almost a decade and, at the time of writing, the final resolution still seems some way off. However, the most striking feature of our evidence on this issue is how little young people differ from their parents – previous surveys of opinion among parent and adult samples have found that those who personally benefitted from the current arrangements tended to support their retention, while those who did not tended to support reform and change. The evidence of the YLT surveys is that pupils in schools think essentially in the same way.

References

Akenson, D.H. (1970) *The Irish Education Experiment: The National System of Education in the Nineteenth Century*, London: Routledge and Kegan Paul.

Akenson, D.H. (1973) *Education and Enmity: The Control of Schooling in Northern Ireland 1920–1950*, London: David and Charles.

Alexander, J. et al. (1998) *An Evaluation of the Craigavon Two-tier System.* (Research Report Series). Bangor: DENI.

Burns Report (2001) *Education for the 21st Century: report of the post primary review group, Northern Ireland*. Bangor: Department of Education.

Costello Report, The (2004) *Future Post-Primary Arrangements in Northern Ireland: Advice from the Post-Primary Review Working Group.* Bangor: DENI.

Department of Education for Northern Ireland (2008) *Every School a Good School: A Policy for School Improvement.*Consultation Document, Bangor: Department of Education.

Gallagher, T. (2004) *Education in Divided Societies*, London: Palgrave/MacMillan.

Gallagher, T. and Smith, A. (2001) The Effects of Selective Education in Northern Ireland. *Education Review*, 15: 1, 74–81.

Gallagher, T. and Smith, A. (2000) *The Effects of the Selective System of Secondary Education in Northern Ireland: Main Report*. Bangor: Department of Education.

Leonard, M. and Davey, C. (2001) *Thoughts on the Eleven-plus*, Belfast: Save the Children.

Lundy, L. (2007) Voice is not enough: Conceptualising Article 12 of the United Nations Convention on the Rights of the Child, *British Educational Research Journal*, 33: 6, 927–42.

Lundy, L. and McEvoy, L. (2007) In the Small Places: Education and Human Rights Culture in Conflict-Affected Societies. In Anthony, G., Morison, J. and McEvoy, K. (Eds.) *Judges, Transition and Human Rights*, Oxford: Oxford University Press.

McEvoy, L. (2007) Beneath the Rhetoric: Policy Approximation and Citizenship Education in Northern Ireland. *Education, Citizenship and Social Justice*, 2: 2, 135–57.

Smith, A. (2003) Citizenship Education in Northern Ireland: Beyond National Identity? *Cambridge Journal of Education*, 33: 1, 15–31.

CHAPTER 6

Young people's thoughts on poverty

Alex Tennant and Marina Monteith

- *In the future in Northern Ireland, firstly I would like to see peace between communities and a more socially and economically fair system with no discrimination.*
- *I would love NI to be sectarian free, for all types of abuse on humans and any living thing to be stopped. I would also like to see the 100,000 children in poverty to be zero but if not possible then lowered.*
- *A caring society where no-one should have to live with being discriminated against or their lives being made unnecessarily hard.*
- *A clean happy place to live in where houses and accommodation are affordable instead of young people living in a life of loans.*
- *Peaceful, better, faster health service, rise in the minimum wage level, housing prices reduced, interest rates reduced.*
- *I feel that no amount of proposals or so called 'promises' from the NI government will have an effect on the state NI is currently in. In the future there may be minor changes but I can't visualise a much better NI.*
- *Feel safe. Jobs available. Happy community. No money for no work i.e. people on the dole should contribute to their community.*
- *A place where money is nothing to worry about and everyone can meet their basic needs.*
- *A society which is tolerant and respectful of all people no matter what they believe or who they are. That all people should have the same access to health care and education. Less poverty, more equal society.*

The quotes above are responses to the following question from the 2007 Young Life and Times (YLT) survey:

The new Assembly has the potential to shape the future for our society. Please say what sort of society you want Northern Ireland to be in the future.

Introduction

For organisations such as Save the Children working to end child poverty in Northern Ireland, the restoration of devolution in May 2007 and the focus on 'bread and butter' issues in politics has opened up new opportunities to lobby and campaign for change. Indeed, within months of the Assembly being reinstated, the Committee for the Office of First Minister and Deputy First Minister launched an Inquiry into child poverty, a reflection of strong cross party support on this issue. Moreover, the Executive's Programme for Government set three child poverty targets. The first two: 'work towards the elimination of child poverty in Northern Ireland by 2020 and reducing child poverty by 50 per cent by 2010' reflect the wider UK government targets to eradicate child poverty, but focussing these specifically on eradicating child poverty *in Northern Ireland*. Given the comparative size of populations, it is possible to meet UK targets without lifting any children out of poverty in Northern Ireland. The specific focus on Northern Ireland in these targets was, therefore, of great significance. The third target: 'Work towards the elimination of severe child poverty by 2012' is the first of its kind in the UK, and reflects a concern to ensure that government actions to end child poverty focus on those in most severe poverty, who have proved least affected by government interventions to date (Adelman et al., 2003; Magadi and Middleton, 2007).

So far – so good. However, the challenge for government over the next three years will be to develop a comprehensive set of programmes to end child poverty and to commit appropriate levels of resources to their implementation. The challenge to NGOs such as Save the Children will be to support this process and keep the pressure on government to make the hard budgetary decisions. As our experience of lobbying at the UK government level has demonstrated, even political leaders with apparently strong personal commitments to ending child poverty, and the power to act, will not do so without evidence that the weight of considerable public opinion is behind them. The UK government to date has been criticised for failing to take the initiative and show strong political leadership by building a wider public consensus about its vision for a society free of poverty. This hesitance is based on concerns about public support and the view that public support for reducing income inequality is superficial (Bamfield, 2005).

Bamfield points out that a consistently high proportion of people in Britain think that the gap between high and low incomes is too great, and this belief is combined with strong support for increased public spending on welfare. This, however, reduces significantly when individual impact on taxation is introduced. If the government is serious about tackling child poverty and meeting child poverty targets, it will need to explore the beliefs of the non-poor population and counter some of the negative stereotyping of the poor in order to create public support for eradication policies. Research by the Fabian Society (2005) revealed that most of society has very little understanding of how material hardship impacts on the lives of children and families. To date the work of building public understanding of the reality of poverty has fallen to the non-governmental organisation sector.

In Northern Ireland the existence of child poverty is more widely recognised by the general public than in Great Britain. Nine out of ten Northern Ireland respondents in a 2007 YouGov survey said that child poverty should be a high priority for the government (Save the Children, 2006). Ensuring that significant public resources are diverted to actions to end child poverty in Northern Ireland will continue to require demonstrably strong public support.

As a child rights organisation which seeks to engage children and young people in campaigning, Save the Children is interested in exploring the perceptions and attitudes of young people in Northern Ireland to child poverty. To this end we commissioned a number of questions on the 2007 YLT survey, the analysis of which forms the basis of this chapter.

The reality of child poverty in Northern Ireland

According to official government figures, almost one in three children in Northern Ireland today live in poverty. This means that 122,000 children (or 29%) are going without basic necessities such as healthy food,* appropriate clothing or a decent home, because their parents can not afford them. Given

---

* Department of Social Development (DSD): *Households Below Average Income 2005–6*. The figures quoted are based on the UK government's relative income measure, after housing costs have been removed. This measure sets a poverty threshold at 60% of the median UK income, equivalised for different family sizes. A basic guide to the measurement of child poverty can be found in Save the Children's Annual *Child Poverty Report 2007*: 57–62.

this is happening in one of the wealthiest countries in the world, these are shocking and shameful facts.

In our *Annual Child Poverty Report 2007*, Save the Children explored the 'what?' and 'how?' of child poverty in Northern Ireland. What is life like for children living in poverty? How does poverty impact on their lives? Drawing together information from a range of sources, the report drew a comprehensive and dreadful picture of the devastating impact that poverty has on children's lives in Northern Ireland.

Poverty impacts on children's health and educational outcomes: compared to non-poor children, poor children are four times more likely to die before the age of twenty (DHSSPS, 2000) and twice as likely to leave school without any qualifications (DENI, 2005). It impacts on their home life and the environment in which they grow up. It results in them missing out on so many experiences and opportunities that are basic to childhood and child development. It consigns many of them to remain in a cycle of poverty which leads them from poverty in childhood, to poverty in adulthood, to becoming a parent of poor children.

Exploring public attitudes to child poverty

What the report was unable to do, was to explain the 'why?' Why does society tolerate so many children growing up in poverty? Is it because it is seen as inevitable, something that cannot be changed? Or is it because of a lack of awareness of the reality of child poverty? Or because of a preoccupation with the politics of managing divisions instead of tackling deepening socio-economic ills? Or is it a reflection of either deep scepticism about or indifference to the reality of child poverty?

The Joseph Rowntree Foundation (JRF) has commissioned a series of studies on public attitudes to poverty, as part of its *Public Interest in Poverty Issues programme* (PIPI). The purpose of PIPI is to further understanding on how to build support for poverty eradication in the UK by building understanding of attitudes to poverty and exploring the implications of these attitudes for communication and change.

One study analysed data from the 2003 British Social Attitudes survey and used cluster analysis to identify two groups with distinctive views about poverty (Park et al., 2007). Regression analysis was then applied to explore the socio-demographic profiles of the two groups. The analysis suggested that the British population was evenly split between the two groups, which were labelled 'liberals' and 'sceptics'.

The 'liberal' group tended to think that there was quite a lot of poverty in Britain, largely caused by social factors. Most agreed that ordinary working people do not get their fair share of the nation's wealth, and that unemployment benefits are too low. Members of this 'liberal group' are more likely to think that Government should redistribute income from the better-off to the less well-off.

The 'sceptical' group tended to believe that there was very little poverty in Britain, and took a very narrow view on what poverty meant. They were most likely to see laziness or lack of will power underpinning why people live in need. They have a clear view that unemployment benefits are too high and do not support redistribution of income to the less well-off.

Park et al. (2007) then looked at the socio-demographic factors that were associated with each of the two groups. They found that a person was more likely to hold liberal views if – among other things – they were young, well educated, had considerable experience of poverty and were not religious.

A second study commissioned by JRF and undertaken by Castell and Thompson examined the barriers to public acceptance of poverty and inequality in the UK. They found a wariness in applying the word 'poverty' to the situation of people in the UK, and a perception that poverty in the UK is the result of bad choices and wrong priorities rather than a social justice issue. Castell and Thompson (2007: 11) write:

attitude)
to poverty

> It was uncomfortable for our groups to even consider poverty; there was a sense of suspicion overhanging all the general discussion of poverty, as though the public are wary of admitting support for alleviating poverty in case their goodwill should be co-opted for political ends, as a result of which they might themselves lose out.

(11)

Both JRF studies demonstrated that attitudes to poverty vary widely and identified a range of socio-demographic factors that appeared to affect an individual's understanding of poverty. This chapter will now analyse responses to a range of questions about poverty included on the 2007 YLT survey to determine what factors impact on young people's attitudes to poverty in Northern Ireland.

Defining child poverty in Northern Ireland

Having engaged a wide range of actors on the issue of child poverty, including children, adult members of the public, political representatives and journalists, Save the Children finds conversations repeatedly coming back to the question of how poverty is defined. This is indeed important, as how one defines poverty will determine how it is measured, the level of poverty identified and the actions required to eradicate it. If, for example, we measure poverty in Northern Ireland using the international definition of absolute poverty, where a person is considered to be experiencing poverty if they are living on less than a dollar a day, we would conclude that poverty did not exist here. Clearly this is not an appropriate measure for developed countries.

Fundamentally poverty means not having enough money to afford the basic necessities of life. While necessities include items essential to survival including food, water and shelter, within developed societies there is general agreement that people need a wider range of things in order to have a decent standard of living. This conception regards poverty as relative to the society in which it is experienced, linking it to social exclusion, as evident in the European Union definition:

> *Persons, families and groups of persons whose resources (material, cultural and social) are so limited as to exclude them from the minimum acceptable way of life in the Member State to which they belong.*

In reality, while most people agree that a person is experiencing poverty if they are going without basic necessities, there is a degree of scepticism about whether poverty truly exists in the UK. As Castell and Thompson point out, the term 'poverty' is associated with the absolute poverty related to developing countries, and many are uncomfortable with using the same term to describe the more relative poverty in the UK, where people at least generally have some basic necessities:

> *In general the attempt to apply 'poverty' to the UK context prompts a certain amount of resistance and reluctance to extend the same kind of sympathy and support to the poor in the UK as to those in the developing countries.*
>
> (Castell and Thompson, 2007: 10)

To explore the degree of consensus among young people in Northern Ireland over the definition of 'poverty', participants were asked the following two questions:

- *Would you say that someone in Northern Ireland was in poverty if they did not have enough to eat and live?*
- *Would you say that someone in Northern Ireland was in poverty if they had enough to eat and live, but not enough to buy other essential items?*

As one might expect, there was strong agreement (92%) that, if people were going without food and the basics they required to live, they would be living in poverty. However, there was much less agreement with the second statement. Only 42 per cent of respondents believed a person to be in poverty if they had enough to eat and live, but not enough to buy other essential items. The large drop-off in respondents agreeing with the second question indicates that around half of young people (48%) equate poverty with only the most extreme conditions. This suggests a high degree of ambivalence over using the term 'poverty' to describe the experience of relative poverty in Northern Ireland where people may have basic items, but not other things they need in order to have a reasonable standard of living.

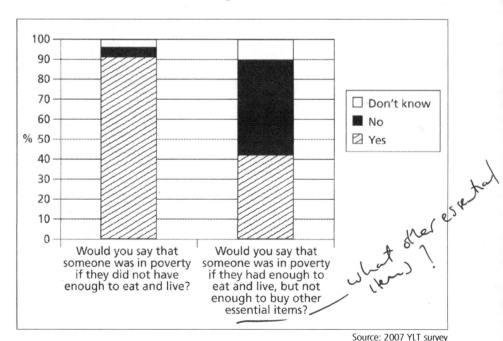

Source: 2007 YLT survey

Figure 6.1 Agreement with definitions of 'poverty'

91

Curiously, four per cent of respondents did not believe that a person who lacked enough to eat and live was in poverty. While in a minority, they present an interesting perspective. It is hard to imagine what would constitute poverty, if not a lack of such basic items. This suggests that there is a small group of young people who are deeply sceptical about the existence of poverty in Northern Ireland. This is consistent with the studies of the adult population referred to previously.

As Table 6.1 shows, there was little variation in responses across a range of socio-demographic characteristics over the first definition of poverty, although there were more differences in response to the second. Even so, the only statistically significant difference was associated with the type of school the respondents last attended. Young people from grammar schools were significantly more likely to consider both scenarios to be poverty. Ninety seven per cent believed a person to be in poverty if they did not have enough to eat and live, compared to 87 per cent of respondents who had attended a secondary school. Furthermore, 53 per cent of grammar school respondents felt a person to be in poverty if they had enough to eat and live, but not enough to buy other essential items, compared to 32 per cent of secondary school pupils.

Defining what is 'essential' for children and young people in Northern Ireland

Respondents were then asked to reflect on whether they considered a number of items to be essential for children and young people in Northern Ireland. These included:

- Three meals a day including fresh fruit and vegetables;
- A television;
- A warm, secure home;
- Being able to participate in social activities outside school;
- A weeks holiday away from home once a year;
- New clothes when needed;
- Educational items such as school books;
- Being able to have a birthday celebration.

As Figure 6.2 indicates, the item that most young people considered to be essential was 'a warm, secure home' – nine in ten (91%) supported this

Compare to PJE

Table 6.1 Definitions of poverty by socio-demographic characteristics

	In poverty if not enough to eat and live?			In poverty if enough to eat and live, but not enough to buy other essential items?		
	Yes	No	Don't know	Yes	No	Don't know
All	92	4	4	42	48	9
Gender						
Male	92	5	2	44	48	8
Female	92	4	4	41	48	9
Place lived						
Urban	97	3	1	50	42	8
Small city or town	91	4	4	37	53	10
Rural	91	5	4	44	45	10
Last school attended						
Grammar	97	3	1	53	40	7
Secondary	87	6	6	32	56	11
Family financial situation						
Not well-off	92	5	4	45	46	8
Average	92	5	3	39	52	9
Well-off	94	2	3	49	41	10
Interest in politics						
Much	94	4	1	53	41	6
Some	95	4	1	45	47	7
Little/none	91	5	5	39	51	11
Community background						
Protestant	91	4	5	37	51	11
Catholic	92	5	3	44	47	9
Neither	97	1	2	45	49	5

Source: 2007 YLT survey

position. While 'three meals a day including fresh fruit and vegetables' was the item next most likely to be described as essential (78%), it was followed closely by 'educational items such as school books' (74%).

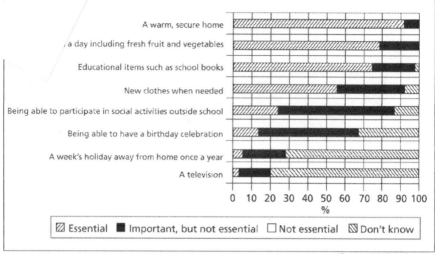

Source: 2007 YLT survey

Figure 6.2 Understanding of whether items are 'essential'

Opinion was more divided on whether 'new clothes when needed' was essential (55%) or merely important (36%). 'Social activities outside school' and 'being able to have a birthday celebration' were much less likely to be considered essential (24% and 14% respectively), although they were still considered by the majority to be important. 'A week's holiday away from home' and 'a television' were considered least essential or important by respondents.

When responses are compared by gender, the order in which these items are prioritised by males and females is consistent, although there are differences in the degree to which each group considers the items to be essential. As can be seen in Figure 6.3, females are more likely to consider 'a warm, secure home', 'three meals a day', and 'educational items' as essential than males. Males are more likely than females to consider 'new clothes when needed'; 'participation in social activities'; 'a birthday celebration', 'a holiday'; and 'a television' as essential.

The type of school attended also appears to reflect a difference in how likely a respondent is to describe an item as 'essential'. In all but one case those from secondary schools were more likely to consider an item essential than those from grammar schools. Indeed, secondary school pupils were the only group with a higher proportion considering 'educational items' essential compared to

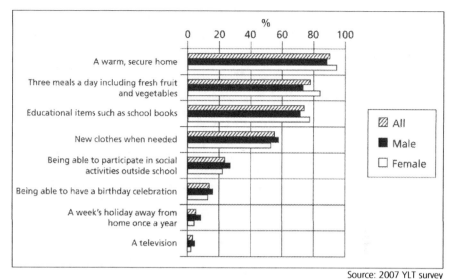

Source: 2007 YLT survey

Figure 6.3 Percentage stating items as essential, by gender

'three meals a day'. The largest differences were in the social development items: 'participating in activities outside school', 'having a birthday celebration' and 'a week's holiday', as Figure 6.4 shows.

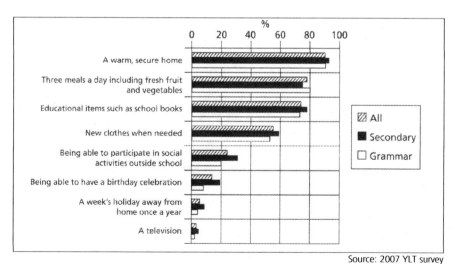

Source: 2007 YLT survey

Figure 6.4 Percentage stating items as essential, by school last attended

The financial situation of the young person's family also seemed to impact on how likely respondents are to consider an item as essential (Figure 6.5). Those describing their family's financial status as 'not well-off' were more likely to consider 'a warm secure home', 'participation in social activities outside the home' and 'a week's holiday' as essential than better-off participants.

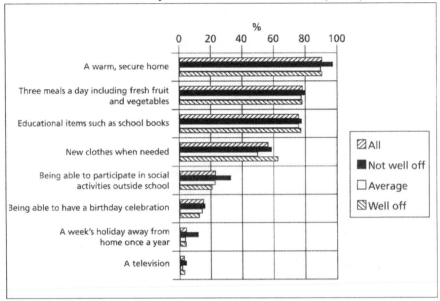

Figure 6.5 Percentage stating items as essential, by family's financial situation

In general, young people were more likely to state as essential those most basic needs of any person – a warm place to live and adequate food to eat. Interestingly other items which high proportions of children stated as essential were items which are most likely to be noticed to be lacking on a daily basis such as educational aids and new clothes. This would confirm that it is important for children and young people that they do not seem different from their peers. Similarly being able to participate in social activities outside of school was more likely to be essential than having a birthday celebration or a week's holiday. This finding replicates the key findings in *Dare to Care* research published in Great Britain in 2007, about which Hilary Fisher commented:

. . . for children it seems the visible indicators of poverty are the ones that they are most sensitive about. Not being able to afford to go on school trips or the correct uniform leads to uncomfortable questions from their peers.

Forthcoming Save the Children research (Monteith and Horgan, 2008), found in discussions with children that decisions about whether an item was essential reflected how often they could participate – or be excluded. Birthday celebrations or holidays, being once-a-year events, were less of a priority whereas not being able to participate in day-to-day social activities incur greater levels of exclusion.

Perceptions of levels of child poverty in Northern Ireland.

The young people surveyed in the 2007 YLT survey were then asked for their opinion on whether there was a little or a lot of child poverty in Northern Ireland. Almost half (45%) felt that there was very little, while a third (31%) felt that there was quite a lot. A significant proportion (24%) opted for 'don't know'.

There was a striking (and statistically significant) difference in responses by gender. Males were twice as likely to opt for 'very little' (53%) rather than 'quite a lot' (26%). Females were much more evenly divided, with 39 per cent believing there to be 'very little' poverty compared to 35 per cent choosing the 'quite a lot' answer option.

Those living in 'not well-off' families perceived there to be higher levels of poverty than those from average or well-off families. This is perhaps unsurprising – one might expect those experiencing poverty to have a heightened awareness of the levels of child poverty in Northern Ireland. Similarly the young people who described themselves as having much interest in politics were more likely to think that there is quite a lot of poverty in Northern Ireland compared to those who said they had 'some', 'little' or 'no interest' (Table 6.2).

This question was adapted from a question asked of 3,272 adults in Great Britain as part of the 2003 British Social Attitudes survey (BSA) – the only difference being that the original question referred to poverty in Britain, as opposed to child poverty in Northern Ireland. In contrast to the response of the

Table 6.2 Perceptions of levels of child poverty in Northern Ireland

	%		
	There is very little poverty	*There is quite a lot poverty*	*Don't know*
All	45	31	24
Gender			
Male	53	26	21
Female	39	35	26
Place lived			
Urban	43	34	23
Small city/town	45	28	27
Rural	48	32	20
Last school attended			
Grammar	46	30	23
Secondary	44	31	25
Family financial background			
Not well-off	39	43	18
Average	47	28	24
Well-off	47	29	23
Interest in politics			
Much interest in politics	42	45	13
Some interest in politics	45	30	25
Little interest/none	47	27	26
Community background			
Protestant	50	22	27
Catholic	40	39	20
Neither	48	30	22

Source: 2007 YLT survey

young people to the YLT survey question, respondents to the 2003 BSA survey were more likely to say that there was 'quite a lot' of poverty (55%), than 'very little' (41%) (Park et al., 2007).

Reaction to levels of child poverty in Northern Ireland.

The 2007 YLT respondents were then presented with the actual number of children living in poverty, along with a simple definition. According to government statistics at the time of designing the survey, just over 100,000 children in Northern Ireland were experiencing poverty – roughly one in four children (24%).* The young people were then asked to indicate which of five statements best described what they thought about the number of children living in poverty in Northern Ireland:

- This is much higher than I thought.
- This is a little higher than I thought.
- This is about as many as I thought.
- This is a little lower than I thought.
- This is much lower than I thought.

Almost nine in ten respondents (88%) said that the figure of 100,000 children in poverty was higher than they had thought, the majority (71%) feeling that it was much higher. Only one per cent felt that it was lower than they had thought. There was remarkably little variation in responses across different socio-demographic groups, with one exception. Table 6.3 shows that compared to young people describing their family's financial situation as 'average' (90%) or 'well-off' (92%), 'not well-off' young people were significantly less likely to say that this was higher than they had thought (79%). Similarly they were more likely to say than other respondents that this was 'lower than they had thought' (7% and 1% respectively).

Even a majority of those who had previously said that they thought that there was quite a lot of child poverty in Northern Ireland said that the official figures were much higher than they had thought (54%). Eighty four per cent of those who had thought that there was very little poverty said that the figures were much higher than they had thought.

---

* Relative income poverty measure using a threshold of 60% median income, equivalised for different family sizes. AHC. DSD, *Households Below Average Income 2005–6*. By the time the questionnaire was in the field, more recent figures had been released, showing that 122,000, or 29% of children were then living in poverty in Northern Ireland.

Table 6.3 Comments on level of child poverty, by family financial background

	Much higher	A little higher	About as many	A little lower	Much lower	Don't know
			%			
All	71	17	6	1	<1	3
Not well-off	64	15	8	5	2	5
Average	72	18	6	1	0	4
Well-off	75	17	7	1	0	1

Source: 2007 YLT survey

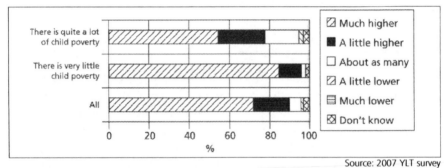

Source: 2007 YLT survey

Figure 6.6 Comments on level of child poverty, by previous perceptions

Support for action to end child poverty

We have seen that young people are surprised by the official figures for child poverty in Northern Ireland, but does this surprise translate into a demand for political action? To test this, we then asked the following two questions:

- *The Northern Ireland Assembly was restored in May of this year. Do you think that child poverty should be a low or high priority for the new Assembly?*
- *In Northern Ireland laws prevent people from being discriminated against, for example because of their age, their religion, their race, and whether they are disabled or not. Do you think that these laws should be changed in order to prevent people from being discriminated against because they are poor?*

Table 6.4 Priority Assembly should place on child poverty, by socio-demographic characteristics

	%			
	High priority	*Neither high nor low priority*	*Low priority*	*Don't know*
All	85	8	2	4
Gender				
Male	82	12	3	3
Female	88	5	2	5
Place lived				
Urban	88	10	1	1
Small city/town	83	8	2	7
Rural	85	8	3	4
Last school attended				
Grammar	85	11	1	3
Secondary	86	5	3	6
Family financial background				
Not well-off	84	8	1	6
Average	88	6	2	3
Well-off	82	13	1	4
Interest in politics				
Much interest in politics	85	11	4	0
Some interest in politics	85	8	3	4
Little interest/no interest in politics	86	7	2	5
Community background				
Protestant	86	8	2	4
Catholic	86	7	3	4
Neither	78	13	3	6

Source: 2007 YLT survey

An overwhelming 85 per cent said that child poverty should be a high priority, and only two per cent felt that it should be a low priority. There was little divergence from this, and young people from Catholic and Protestant background were equally supportive of making child poverty a high priority.

Females were slightly more likely to say that child poverty should be a high priority than males.

There was also strong support for putting in place legislation to prevent discrimination associated with poverty, with almost three in four respondents agreeing (74%). As shown in Figure 6.7, those describing themselves as 'not well off' were more likely to agree with this (80%) than young people describing their family's financial situation as 'average' (74%) or 'well-off' (70%).

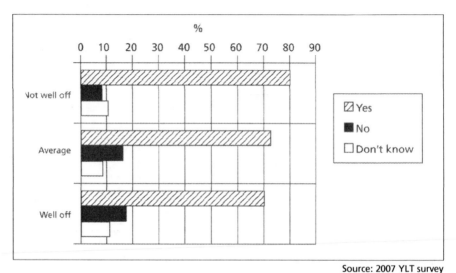

Source: 2007 YLT survey

Figure 6.7: Support for legislation to prevent discrimination by poverty. By financial situation of family

Unlike the previous question, the level of support was not consistent for young people from Protestant and Catholic backgrounds. While a majority of young people from Protestant backgrounds supported putting in place legislation to prevent people being discriminated against because they are poor (64%), the support was significantly higher among young people from Catholic backgrounds (83%).

Indeed, as Figure 6.8 shows, there was little difference among young people from Catholic backgrounds in support for the two actions suggested – prioritising child poverty and putting in place legislation to prevent discrimination on the grounds of poverty. This was also the case for young people who described their community background as neither Catholic nor Protestant. In contrast, among young people from Protestant backgrounds there was a significant difference in support for the two actions suggested. This finding reflects historical differences in how human rights and equality legislation has been viewed by political parties representing the two main socio-religious communities in Northern Ireland. The fact that still a majority of Protestant 16-year olds in the 2007 YLT survey support legislation to prevent discrimination by poverty may suggest a different perspective amongst these young people than the political parties claiming to represent their community.

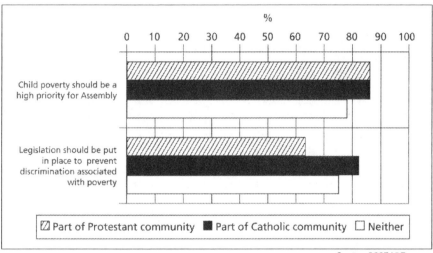

Source: 2007 YLT survey

Figure 6.8 Support for actions on child poverty, by community background

Conclusions

This chapter explored young people's attitudes to poverty in Northern Ireland, and how these attitudes are related to both socio-demographic factors and 16-year-olds' experiences of being poor. In relation to the question on how poverty should be defined, YLT respondents were evenly split between those who applied the term 'poverty' only to those who lacked enough to eat and live, and those who would also apply it to people going without other essential items. However, overall there was a strong consensus in support of action by government to end child poverty, with 85 per cent saying that child poverty should be made a high priority by the Assembly.

Analysis of the 2007 YLT survey shows that young people's perceptions and opinions of child poverty in Northern Ireland are affected by their own background and experiences. Most strikingly, young people who come from a low income families are more likely than young people from wealthier backgrounds to be aware of the prevalence of poverty and to feel more strongly that poverty needs to be addressed. However, it is important to emphasise that there was strong overall support for action on child poverty amongst all YLT respondents.

Committed political leadership will be required over the next few years to ensure that the Northern Ireland Executive meets its targets of halving child poverty by 2010, and eradicating severe child poverty by 2012. For organisations such as Save the Children who seek to engage young people in campaigning to ensure government meets its commitments this analysis provides a useful insight, and evidence of strong support for action. While a significant proportion of young people were not initially entirely comfortable with using the term 'poverty' to describe anything other than absolute poverty, this ambivalence over the term seemed to diminish on working through a number of challenging questions on the issue. The actual level of child poverty in Northern Ireland appears to have surprised most young people and contributed to strong support for government action to end child poverty.

Save the Children believes that a comprehensive dialogue needs to take place between government and civil society on how child poverty can be effectively tackled. This study has demonstrated that it is particularly important to include young people in this debate.

For more information on Save the Children's campaign to end child poverty and on how you can get involved, visit www.savethechildren.org.uk/northernireland

References

Adelman, L., Middleton, S. and Ashworth, K. (2003) *Britain's Poorest Children: Severe and Persistent Poverty and Social Exclusion*, London: Save the Children.

Bamfield, L. (2005) *Making the Public Case for Tackling Poverty and Inequality.* London: CPAG Poverty Magazine, Issue 121.

Castell, S. and Thompson, J. (2007) *Understanding Attitudes to Poverty in the UK: Getting the Public's Attention.* York: Joseph Rowntree Foundation.

Committee for the Office of First Minister and Deputy First Minister (2008) *Interim Report of the Inquiry into Child Poverty.* Belfast: Northern Ireland Assembly.

Dare to Care (2007): *Missing School Trips makes you Poor – say British kids.* Press release 19 September 2007. London: Dare to Care.

DENI (Department for Education for Northern Ireland) (2005) *Northern Ireland School Leavers Survey 2004/5.* Belfast, DENI.

Department for Social Development (2007) *Households Below Average Income 2005–6.* Belfast: DSD.

DHSSPS (2000) *Investing in Health: Consultation Document.* Belfast: DHSSPS.

Fabian Society (2005) *Why Life Chances Matter? The Interim Report of the Fabian Commission on Life Chances and Child Poverty.* London: Fabian Society.

Magadi, M. and Middleton, S. (2007) *Severe Child Poverty in the UK.* London: Save the Children.

Monteith, M. and Horgan, G. (2008) *A Framework for Child Poverty Indicators: The Children and Young People's Perspective.* London: Save the Children.

Northern Ireland Executive (2008) *Programme for Government 2008–2011.* Belfast: OFMDFM.

Park, A., Phillips, M. and Robinson, C. (2007) *Attitudes to Poverty: Findings from the British Social Attitudes Survey.* York: Joseph Rowntree Foundation.

Save the Children (2006) *Getting on Track for 2020.* Belfast: Save the Children.

Save the Children (2007) *State of Child Poverty in Northern Ireland 2007.* Belfast: Save the Children.

CHAPTER 7

Is anybody listening?*

Shaun Mulvenna

They say the most important part of a story is the first few lines, and most writers today have perfected the art of capturing the reader's attention.

So how am I going to set about writing an essay, which will captivate you all from start to finish? After all I do not want this essay to end up shoved in some old cupboard never to see daylight again. No, I want everyone, grown ups in particular, to hear all about the lives and times of young people in Northern Ireland today . . . What? You're interested? Yes, I thought you might be, because it seems those who don't inhabit our emerald isle hold the opinion that Northern Ireland is a war zone, a blemish on the map of the world, and as for the under 18s, why, they should all be gathered up and transported to a remote island (preferably without food and water) and left there. After all, we are nothing more than a bunch of abusive, aggressive and brainless animals that would not look out of place alongside the monkeys in Belfast Zoo. Aren't we?

Well believe it our not, we don't all mug grannies in the street or leave our chewing gum on the cinema seats. Some of us even put it in the bin (don't look so surprised!). Yes, I feel we youths have a hard time in this modern day and age. Do not mistake me for the moody 16-year-old who answers in grunts and complains that I need more 'space'. No, I speak for all those people who are misjudged and misunderstood and most offensive of all, misrepresented. I am not defending the lost causes that are the explanation to the graffiti on walls, the tangled swings in the park or the increase in cigarette sales. The only positive aspect is, that these people are in the minority.

---

* This is the winning essay from a competition that ran alongside the 2007 YLT survey. All YLT respondents and 16-year-old pupils attending post-primary schools were invited to write an essay on the subject of *The Lives and Times of Young People in Northern Ireland Today.*

The rest of us are sent to the 'lunatic asylum', the grey haired ones like to call 'school'. Over the years I have mastered the art of eating my toast and marmalade whilst pulling on my trousers and running for the bus all at the same time. As for the journey, well it is no plain sailing, free seats these days are a luxury and I highly doubt those scrawny seats were designed to hold two people, never mind three extra (many of whom are not . . . shall we say 'strangers' to a McDonalds 'Big Mac').

However, I dare not mention this to anyone who was old enough to remember England winning the World Cup (a long, long . . . long time ago) because I know I will be met by a thick ear and the lecture I have heard all too many times, how the old fogies; 'were made to walk ten miles to school, barefoot, come rain hail or snow!' No, mastering the art of sitting on an 'edge' is a feat in itself. Perching on a prefabricated seat would bring tears to the eyes of even the most hardened of travellers.

One thing I constantly puzzle over during my trips to school is why Northern Irish athletes rarely feature in the weight lifting contests at the Olympics. I feel that with the weight of the modern day bag (around the same load as a new born elephant) we could give any Russian strongman a run for their money. Who needs gym membership when you own a schoolbag!

We 16-year-olds don't have it easy in school either. The teachers may as well brand the letters GCSEs onto our foreheads with a hot iron! There is no time for eating or sleeping, it's work, work, work! It would seem the only people who prosper at this time of the year are the shopkeepers who can expect an increase in sales of red bull and coffee for all those late night studiers.

As well as balancing school life with household chores (yes, we *can* actually work a vacuum cleaner!) most of us have part time jobs. And to think you had the cheek to call us lazy! The next time you order a meal or buy your frozen curry, take a look at the polite teenager in front of you, slaving away for £3.45 an hour. No wonder most employers these days look so happy. Pocketing half our wages whilst doing minimal work . . . what a life!

Our one escape from the trials and tribulations of school life and part time work can be found in the form of the glorious Internet. Not only can we numb our brains by playing pointless (but extremely enjoyable) games but also we can gossip to our mates on chat rooms, which unlike an hour on the phone, doesn't cost quite as much. Anything to save a grilling from the parents! Yes MSN, Face Book, and My Space have become a favourite for teenagers everywhere, however the number one website for creating a 'virtual you' would have to be Bebo. At the very mention of the word I can almost hear the grown ups tearing out their hair. It means hours spent trying to wrench your child from the computer (believe me, I have been the rope in the tug of war!).

The ancient ones simply haven't realised just how important this website is. It allows us to talk to our friends whether we are two houses away or in different countries and yes, I admit it is hard to keep your conversations private when they are broadcasted for all to see but when it comes down to it . . . we don't care!

Bebo basically allows you to create a page all about yourself with a section showing your top 16 friends, your uploaded videos, the groups you have joined (in my case a page dedicated to Manchester United) and any other important information you wish to include. I am saying this to inform all you adults out there because it would be easier to find a fire-breathing dog with nine legs than a young person who doesn't know about Bebo. I agree that there are a select few out there who abuse the site by using it to bully but these are the same people who turn pencils into dangerous weapons and put fireworks through your letterboxes . . . idiots in other words. They exist in every walk of society, and just because they misuse the site doesn't mean it should be banned for everyone else. You simply have to log on and explore to find tribute pages to victims of cancer, road accidents, and natural disasters. So there, we aren't all a bunch of scandal loving gossips!

As well as being criticised for being lazy, violent, moody (the list goes on), it seems even our very dress sense is being frowned upon. I ask you, what is wrong with the 'hoodie'? Surely you have realised that the fashion industry has moved on and woolly cardigans with matching caps aren't exactly the latest fashion. Which brings me to another point; designer clothing! So much pressure is put on teenagers in Northern Ireland today to have the latest Nike trainers or the most expensive Replay jeans. Large companies take advantage raising the prices higher and higher, its daylight robbery and nobody will do anything about it.

Phew! I think I have put across just a *few* of the many hurdles we 16-year-olds must overcome in our quest for adulthood, but believe it or not, it's not all bad. They say, 'Life begins at forty'. Of course it doesn't! That saying is for the man who looks in the mirror and discovers a balding patch and a few extra wrinkles, yet reassures himself all is not lost. No, life begins at 16. It is then we open our eyes to the world (once we have slept in till one in the afternoon that is!).

At 16 we are young adults, the future bankers, milkmen, and shopkeepers. (Don't look so afraid.) I am glad to say some adults realise this and slowly but surely start to treat us with a little more respect and value. I am sure I not only speak for myself when I say we begin to appreciate more in our lives. In my case, I look forward to nothing more than getting up at seven in the morning, to get a bus up to Lisburn to play football. This simple pleasure makes up for the growing amount of maths homework and the dirty looks from pensioners!

Even in my own school there are simple pleasures to be found. Past the dungeon like classrooms where the geography teacher jabs dangerously at the map, beyond the perplexed maths tutor who struggles over one of his own questions, there is hope in the form of friends. Friends who will give us a ham sandwich when our mum has made cheese. Friends who let us copy their homework (let's face it, we all do it!) when we leave our own on the bus. Friends who will always pass the ball, even if we play like an elderly donkey. Yes, they are the ones who make certainly my school life a lot more bearable, because without them, it all seems too much to bear.

For this reason, I feel particularly sorry for those people the same age as myself who don't have a mate or companion, because they are more likely to be targeted by bullies. Even in my very own school, in the very middle of the countryside, there are people who aren't happy until they've made someone else's day miserable. Why do they do it? The answer: a difference in appearance, looks or even accent. Little things, that should no longer matter. However, how many of us, myself included, can say we would jump in and stop this? The numbers wouldn't exactly put a smile on your face. The reason? We don't want to interfere in case the abuse is redirected towards ourselves. For most 16-year-olds in Northern Ireland, keeping in with your crowd matters, and most of us steer clear of anything that could jeopardise this.

Another topic that creates tension between teenagers in Northern Ireland is religion. The old Catholic, Protestant; Celtic, Rangers; Linfield, Glentoran argument. Being from a mixed village I never really caught on to the hatred between the two sides until I went to my first football training session and witnessed a boy being sent home for wearing Celtic socks. At the time I thought, yes those socks are bright, not something you would parade on the catwalk but were they really that shocking to justify being sent home for? The thought did not occur that those socks could have led to a fight amongst my team members, and the one thing the coach was trying to promote was religious integration. Times have moved on however, slowly . . . very, very slowly but even within my team, I have noticed subtle changes. Any shirts of this sort are banned, and the only fighting that takes place, is over the last Jaffa Cake at half time!

Well up to now, I have tried my best to alter your view on those who are a long way off reaching your prehistoric age. Next time you go to tip the waitress a measly £1.25, shout at those youths for kicking their ball into your petunias, or whinge to your friend about how the Internet is ruining the children of today, take a step back. They have enough problems such as school, relationships and 'the parents' without having to worry about everyone else. Teenage life isn't simply a thick slice of happiness with a garnish of fun. In Northern Ireland however, for the first time in many years, we adolescents have a bright future to look forward to. Let's go for it!

CHAPTER 8

Giving young people a voice via social research projects: methodological challenges

Dirk Schubotz and Paula Devine

I think Young Life and Times is a very good opportunity for young people to get their views taken into perspective.

(YLT respondent, 2003)

Introduction

In recent years there has been an increasing recognition that social research into children's and young people's issues should not just be undertaken for its own sake or just in order to further the academic career of those undertaking the research. Rather there is an acknowledgement that empirical social researchers carry an ethical responsibility to listen to participants in the research and to feed back results to policy makers and informants. 'Participation' and 'consultation' are two relatively new but significant concepts that have entered into the jargon of empirical social research. It is now regarded as good practice for funders of social research projects to require clear statements on how structures are put in place that ensure that consultation and participation are comprehensive and not tokenistic. The research dissemination strategy often involves seminars open to the public, press releases and lay-friendly summaries of key findings.

Regardless of their academic affiliation, the size of their project and their institution, the growth of the World-wide Web has given researchers the opportunity to share information to an extent that is well beyond what was even imaginable just 25 years ago. However, whilst the technical conditions are now in place to make research information available to anyone who really cares about it, the insight among some researchers that knowledge transfer with the public is ethically desirable may lag somewhat behind these technical advances.

Within this context, ARK was set up by social researchers of the two Northern Ireland universities in 2000. From its onset the project had the single goal 'to make social and political information on Northern Ireland available to the widest possible audience'. ARK is largely a web-based resource, even though direct interaction with the public through seminars and other events also take place. From day one of the project, ARK followed a dissemination strategy which was directed at a broad audience, including researchers, policy makers, journalists, community and voluntary groups, schoolchildren, teachers – in fact anyone with an interest in social issues in Northern Ireland. Thus, ARK provides *Access* to, *Research* on, and *Knowledge* about Northern Ireland's social and political affairs in the broadest sense.

YLT: listening to children and young people

Young Life and Times (YLT) is a constituent part of ARK and therefore shares the same ethos in relation to making information available. As a project focusing on young people, YLT is committed to the aims of the United Nations' *Convention on the Rights of the Child* (UNCRC, 1989), which states in Article 12 that:

> *State parties shall assure to the child who is capable of forming his or her own views the right to express those views freely in all matters affecting the child, the views of the child being given due weight in accordance with the age and maturity of the child.*

In Northern Ireland, the Children (NI) Order 1995, and, most recently, the Ten Year Strategy for Children and Young People in Northern Ireland, 2006–2016 endorse and recognise the right of children and young people to be consulted and listened to in matters affecting them.

For researchers involved in the YLT project, these statutory commitments to listen to, and consult with, young people is both an opportunity and a challenge at the same time. It gives us the chance to develop a research instrument that is independent but at the same time relevant. However, if we want to take ourselves seriously, we will need to be ready to be measured against ARK's mission to make information available whilst ensuring that this information is being used in the interests of the 16-year olds who we invite to take part in our research. Ultimately this means we have to strive to develop a research instrument that is state of the art both academically and methodologically, as well as in relation to participatory standards. This research instrument is the Young Life and Times survey.

Awareness of the UNCRC and experiences of being consulted

Twice in its existence, the YLT survey has asked respondents whether they were aware of the UNCRC. In the first YLT survey in 1998, only one quarter of respondents (25%) said they had ever heard of the UNCRC. At the time, YLT ran alongside the Northern Ireland Life and Times (NILT) survey and included all 12–17-year olds living in the households of adult respondents (see Appendix 1 of this book for more details). NILT respondents were also asked the same question. Again the level of awareness among NILT respondents was fairly low (36%), although it was significantly higher than among YLT respondents. However, the vast majority of respondents to both surveys in 1998 (80% of YLT respondents and 88% of NILT respondents) felt that children and young people had more opportunities to express their views than young people had 20 years ago. Nevertheless, 84 per cent of YLT respondents still felt that they should be given even *more* opportunity to express their views. In addition, only 15 per cent of YLT respondents felt that they had been given 'a lot' of opportunity in their school to express their view and less than one third (31%) had *ever* been asked their opinion on how something was run in their school. Only 16 per cent of respondents felt that they had helped change the way something was run in their school by expressing their view.

The question on the awareness of the UNCRC was repeated in NILT in 2002, and the level of awareness was a little higher then (43%) than in 1998. Using the current YLT sampling frame, a random sample of 16-year-olds were asked in 2007 whether they had ever heard of the UNCRC. Just over one quarter (28%) said that they had.

In Chapter 3 of this book, Ruth Sinclair writes about the challenges of involving children and young people in decision-making in school. The YLT data would certainly suggest that in terms of awareness-raising on the rights of children and young people, including the right to be heard and listened to, not much progress has been made in the last decade.

Listening to young people: methodological challenges

For the YLT team, the ambition to make young people's voices heard and listened to by policy makers poses a number of challenges. The annual YLT survey remains our main research instrument and has both advantages and disadvantages. As a means of asking young people their opinions on issues that affect them, the use of a large-scale survey can be restrictive, with some obvious limitations:

- The majority of questions are asked because researchers *think* they should be asked and anticipate that they are relevant to respondents, or – if they are not – that respondents are still willing to cooperate and complete the questions.
- The majority of questions are closed, that is, the answer options are also anticipated and categorised by researchers prior to the fieldwork.
- Survey questionnaires do not generally provide means of exploring certain issues in depth and so can be inflexible.

However, running an annual YLT survey has also obvious benefits. Aside from the survey's generalisability and comparative value, the main advantage of the annual format of the YLT survey is the ability to follow trends over time, which for policy makers is an important feature to measure the impact of policy interventions. Katrina Lloyd, Ed Cairns, Claire Doherty and Kate Ellis use this facility in Chapter 2 of this book in their discussion of the timely and sensitive subject area of mental health. They show that an increase in the suicide rate among young people since the cessation of paramilitary violence in Northern Ireland does not appear to be a reflection of a deterioration in mental health of young people overall. In relation to the governmental suicide prevention strategy (DHSSPS, 2006), this is very useful information.

Similarly, Duncan Morrow in Chapter 1 of this volume uses YLT time-series data on attitudes to community relations to draw conclusions for the tasks of the Community Relations Council, the agency for which he is Chief Executive. Again, from his point of view, researching changing attitudes to community relations and cross-community contact among young people who belong to the first post-conflict generation gives his agency important messages to inform the work they are undertaking.

However, Duncan Morrow also combines the YLT time-series data with comments from respondents to an open question in the YLT survey, which was asked for the first time in 2003:

Is there anything else that you would like to say about community relations in Northern Ireland?

When we received the completed questionnaires, we were taken aback by how many young people had taken the opportunity to comment on their feelings and thoughts on community relations and what length, depth and quality most of these comments had. Thus, the question has been asked ever since, and each year about one third of all respondents have used the opportunity to assert their views.

Perhaps the huge amount of qualitative data collected on this topic through the YLT surveys is evidence for how important an issue community relations remain to be in Northern Ireland, as Duncan Morrow also concluded in his chapter. Sometimes however, these comments went well beyond the immediate issue of community relations, as the two examples below exemplify:

To be blunt it is rubbish, it's not just religion that people don't understand, there is also sexuality, other cultures and everything that other countries have moved on with in the last 50 years. Living in this country is like living in 1952, utterly ridiculous. It all happens because people don't understand. No one teaches that being homosexual is okay and not a choice. No one teaches that there are different religions in the world, that people of the other religion live in this country and that everyone's entitled to their own beliefs. No one teaches that you have to grow up and be mature about things if you want to survive in a world outside Northern Ireland. No one teaches the fact that people express themselves in different ways. When religious education is taught at school they don't teach anything other than Christianity. Community relations are quite pathetic.

(YLT respondent, 2003)

I believe that in some areas, young people are so bored they stir trouble just for something to do. For a 'kick'. If the government provided more for them to do, I believe such problems could be avoided. For instance, if I were to see a new play park being built, my first reaction would be 'in no time thugs would have it destroyed' which is based on past experiences. More logical distractions from violence such as grants for cinemas etc. should be thought about. I also believe that there are more problems than religious ones for teenagers to the concerned about. Being a victim of stereotype can be stressful. Getting labelled as an 'emo' or a 'jock' or a 'Barbie' can cause stress when really I believe those teens only conform to such images to get a sense of belonging and worth.

(YLT respondent, 2003)

Methodologically, the hundreds of comments we have received each year were encouragement and evidence that a large-scale survey like YLT, at least to some degree, could also be used as a vehicle to collect more in-depth information that can be used to inform policy making in consultation on young people's issues.

We took this willingness from YLT respondents to reply comprehensively to the open question on community relations in Northern Ireland as an encouragement to include more open questions on other subject areas when we felt this was appropriate. For example, in the 2005 YLT survey we asked respondents about their experiences of and attitudes towards health adverse behaviours (drinking alcohol, taking drugs and smoking) as well as experiences of sexual intercourse. The question had the same format as the question on community relations. We asked:

Is there anything else you would like to say about smoking, drinking, drugs and sexual matters?

Again we received hundreds of responses which were just as diverse and captivating as the comments on community relations. Simon Blake uses some of these comments in his chapter which underpin the quantitative evidence he presents on sexual health work for young people.

Another open question we asked in the survey was: *What makes you stressed?* (YLT, 2004 and 2005). Whilst Katrina Lloyd and her co-authors do not quote any actual replies to this question in their chapter in this volume, they present a table on the quantified responses to this question in tabular format and relate this to the mental health question they are discussing.

More recently, we have also included three open questions in the YLT surveys that were directly related to policy making on young people. In 2005, we asked:

If the government decided that they should be spending more money on young people in Northern Ireland, how do you think they should spend the extra money?

In the latest YLT survey (2007) we asked respondents to name up to three issues that they felt should be a high priority for the Northern Ireland Assembly. We also asked:

The new Assembly has the potential to shape the future for our society. Please use the space below to say what sort of society you want Northern Ireland to be in the future.

We will present the responses to this question to the new Northern Ireland Executive.

The 2007 survey is perhaps the most direct example so far of how the YLT survey has been used in order elicit young people's voices and inform policy making. The questions above were asked on behalf of Save the Children who had placed a module on attitudes to and experiences of child poverty and children's rights in the YLT survey. Alex Tennant and Marina Monteith report findings of this module in Chapter 6. Their organisation also lobbied the Northern Ireland Executive and Assembly with findings of the YLT survey to raise awareness of the ongoing issue of child poverty.

Findings reported by Ruth Sinclair in Chapter 3 also stem from a direct cooperation of the National Children's Bureau (NCB) with YLT on the issue of school bullying and involvement of young people in decision making and policy making in schools (Schubotz and Sinclair et al., 2006; NICCY, 2006). Tony Gallagher also refers to some of these results in his chapter. Despite these successful collaborations, it is important to highlight that YLT is not an omnibus survey in the traditional sense, and the researchers involved in YLT maintain autonomy in their decision on what questions will be asked and what wording will be used, hence assuring academic integrity of the project.

The methodological advantages of asking the same questions year by year have already been highlighted above. However, we also feel that YLT has responsibility of assuring that survey questions asked mirror societal changes. This can present problems as a change in question wording means that time-series and longitudinal data analyses are restricted. YLT has tried to find the right balance in asking timely questions that relate to young people's issues and reflect the changes in society on the one hand whilst providing a long-term analytical framework for researchers and practitioners that wish to use the YLT data, on the other. Two examples should illustrate this.

Firstly, since their beginning, both the NILT and YLT surveys recorded data on the ethnic background of respondents. In the early surveys we used a question which was based on the Census of Population. However, we found that the available answer categories were partly contradictory and partly did not reflect the complex realities of identity formation. After careful consultation we altered this question and since 2005 we simply ask the open question:

To which ethnic group do you consider you belong?

Whilst the responses may pose new questions and data analysis remains challenging, we feel that we now ask the most appropriate question in relation to ethnic identity formation which shows that religiosity, race, language and national identity all impact on ethnic identity of young people. The following examples of responses, all taken from the 2006 YLT survey, to the question clearly indicate these complexities:

- White/Caucasian
- White Roman Catholic
- White Irish
- White European
- Protestant Northern Irish
- Mixed race
- Presbyterian
- Ulster Protestant
- European, White, Christian
- English/Indian
- Asian
- I don't know

Secondly, one of the most difficult questions to ask in survey questionnaires is that of sexual identity because it often yields relatively large proportions of refusals and/or unreliable answers. NILT has been asking respondents whether they were 'gay or lesbian (homosexual)', 'heterosexual or straight' or 'bisexual' since 2000. In the latest available NILT survey (2006), less than one per cent of respondents said they were 'gay or lesbian' or 'bisexual'. Ninety-eight per cent said they were heterosexual and two per cent refused to answers this question. This result is clearly a stark under-representation of non-heterosexual people in the population and suggests that respondents feel uncomfortable answering this question in this way. Of course Northern Ireland has a tradition of being uncomfortable with the issue of sexuality, which is evident from its exclusion from the British National Surveys of Sexual Attitudes and Lifestyles (Erens et al., 2003; Johnson et al., 1994; 2001; Wellings et al., 2001). Beyond stating this lack of comfort and the obvious unreliability of the responses, the question asked on sexual identity in NILT is unfortunately of limited use for any statistical analysis which may inform policy making on equality issues.

Thus, when we introduced a question on sexual identity in YLT from 2005 onwards, we used the much more subtle question format used in the NATSAL studies and piloted in a sexual attitude and lifestyle survey of young people in Northern Ireland (Schubotz, Simpson and Rolston, 2002). This question asks whether people have ever been sexually attracted to anyone and gives a range of answer options ranging from exclusively heterosexual attraction to exclusively homosexual attraction, as well as the opportunity to say that the respondent was never sexually attracted at all. The results to the YLT surveys have indicated that eight to eleven per cent of respondents have been attracted to a person of the same sex at least once. This figure accurately reflects estimations of the size of the gay, lesbian and bisexual community. Using this data, we have been able to relate same/both-sex attraction with the extent of experienced school bullying, poor school experiences and subsequently poor mental health, which we fed into policy and academic discussions (McNamee, Schubotz and Lloyd, 2008).

One of the main ways of ensuring that we produce YLT survey questionnaires that are interesting and relevant to 16-year-olds is by asking respondents what questions they think we should include in the next year's survey. Each year we include up to five issues raised, with the only restriction being the length of the questionnaire.

Developing participatory research beyond the YLT survey

As we have indicated above, we use a number of methods to ensure that the YLT questionnaire is academically sound, interesting and relevant to participants in the research, whilst also being informative to policy makers. However, this does not take away from the fact that a survey is mainly unsuitable for truly participatory research. In the recent past we have therefore collaborated with other researchers to develop qualitative follow-up projects to the YLT survey in which young people are directly involved.

The first such project was *Voices Behind the Statistics* (Ewart and Schubotz, et al., 2004), which researched young people's views on sectarianism. In this project, interactive participatory focus group discussions were held in schools to elicit views that could not be captured by the YLT survey.

Another project, like the previous one undertaken in conjunction with the National Children's Bureau (NCB), is the one described in length by Ruth Sinclair in Chapter 3 of this book. Again, interactive participatory focus groups were at the core of this project, although one-to-one interviews and additional survey questionnaires were also employed as means of collecting data. What was new in this project was that peer researchers were employed, such that young people were directly involved as junior researchers in the project.

In conjunction with the 2007 YLT survey, a study on community-based community relations projects was initiated (Schubotz and McCarten, 2008). As above, peer researchers were trained and employed to work alongside us in this project. However, we recruited 16-year-olds who had previously taken part in the 2007 YLT survey and who were themselves actively involved in cross-community projects at the time they completed the YLT questionnaire, hence making this project a true follow-up.

In 2007, we also ran an essay-writing competition – yet another means of making young people's voices heard. The winning essay from Shaun Mulvenna, who also took part in the 2007 YLT survey, is published in this book (Chapter 7).

Future plans include mixed-methods projects on experiences of and attitudes to minority ethnic communities, more in-depth explorations of mental health issues and explorations of citizenship and participation. We are also hoping to relate some of these issues more closely to the questions asked in NILT in order to inform policy makers about the similarities and differences between the adult and the youth population in these subject areas.

Conclusions

Each year when we write out to 16-year-olds inviting them to take part in the YLT survey, we start our letter to them with the following sentence:

All too often the opinions of young people are ignored when decisions are made about many issues involving them.

YLT as a project set out to listen to young people and to make their voices heard using a particular grounded research methodology. This book project evolved from our desire to disseminate widely some of the best examples of how YLT data has influenced policy making and is continuing to do so. Whilst we remain modest about the generalisability of the data collected in a relatively small and unique part of the United Kingdom and the island of Ireland, we are confident that the YLT approach can be seen as good research practice. In this respect, we believe, that the contributions of the authors in this book have relevance beyond the closely-knit Northern Irish community.

The central aim of ARK is to make social and political information available to the widest possible audience. We do know that a wide international audience of policy makers, politicians, government, researchers and students do use the YLT data we produce. In line with our ethos, we do not limit the access to our website and do not ask for registrations, which can be seen as a boundary to using the website. Due to this open-access policy we can never be completely sure *who* accesses and uses the information. However, we know that the number of visitors on the YLT website, where all the information related to the project is available, has steadily increased to an average between 10,000 and 12,000 visitors per month and has peaked at 17,662 page down loads at the time this book was printed (May 2008).

By no means do we see our mission as accomplished, and the growing wariness about the use of research data and database information in general, which we share to some extent, poses new challenges. Similar to many other social surveys, we have recently seen a steady, albeit small, drop in the return rate in our annual YLT survey. In order to maintain the survey as a relevant research instrument, we need to think about ways of ensuring that young people remain convinced that taking part in our research will benefit them and/or the younger generation.

Giving a feedback of key findings of the research to participants is only the first and smallest step, and we have consistently done this since 2003. However, we have an ethical responsibility to ask timely and relevant questions and use all channels available to us to communicate key findings to decision makers and policy makers. One of our latest developments is ARK in Schools, a web-based resource which offers secondary level pupils tailor-made resources to explore topics that were included in YLT surveys. In a way this is also a method of feeding back information and asking young people to avail themselves of this opportunity does develop notions of active citizenship. In the end, our main role remains to be researchers. This is where we are most skilled. However, if our project can raise awareness among 16-year-olds and encourages them to review their positions, we can truly say that we have developed a participatory and emancipatory project:

> *I would firstly like to thank you for keeping me informed on the 2006 Young Life and Times Survey (. . .) I will visit the YLT website to look at the results as this survey has really made me interested in other young people's school life and how much it differentiates from my own, and it has also given me the ability to see that not all schools are like my own and it has really made me think.*

> (2006 YLT respondent, email response to invitation to attend YLT results launch)

References

ARK. Young Life and Times Survey (1998–2000, 2003–2007) [computer files]. ARK: www.ark.ac.uk/ylt [Accessed 31 January 2008].

ARK. Northern Ireland Life and Times Surveys (1998–2006) [computer files]. ARK: www.ark.ac.uk/nilt [Accessed 31 January 2008].

Department of Health, Social Services and Public Safety (2006) *Draft Suicide Prevention Strategy, Protect Life – A Shared Vision.* Belfast: DHSSPS.

Erens, B. et al. (2003) *National Survey of Sexual Attitudes and Lifestyles II: Reference Tables and Summary Report.* London: National Centre for Social Research.

Ewart, S. and Schubotz, D. et al. (2004) *Voices Behind the Statistics. Young People's Views of Sectarianism in Northern Ireland.* London: NCB.

Johnson, A.M. et al. (2001) Sexual Behaviour in Britain: Partnerships, Practices, and HIV Risk Behaviours. *Lancet,* 358, 1835–42.

Johnson, A.M. et al. (1994) *Sexual Attitudes and Lifestyles.* Oxford: Blackwell Scientific Publications.

McNamee, H., Schubotz, D. and Lloyd, K. (2008) Same Sex Attraction, Homophobic Bullying and Mental Health of Young People in Northern Ireland. *Journal of Youth Studies,* 11: 1, 33–46.

NICCY (2006): *Having Your Say in Bullying Policies. Guidance to Promote the Involvement of Pupils in Anti-bullying School Policies*. Belfast: NICCY (Northern Ireland Commissioner for Children and Young People).

Schubotz, D. and McCarten, C. (2008) *Cross-community Schemes: Participation, Motivation, Mandate*. ARK Research Update 55. Belfast: ARK Publications. Available online at: www.ark.ac.uk/publications/updates/update55.pdf [accessed May 2008].

Schubotz, D., Simpson, A. and Rolston, W.J. (2002) *Towards Better Sexual Health. A Survey of Sexual Attitudes and Lifestyles of Young People in Northern Ireland*. London: fpa.

Schubotz, D. and Sinclair, R. et al. (2006): *Being Part and Parcel of the School. The Views and Experiences of Children and Young People in Relation to the Development of Bullying Policies in Schools*. Belfast: NICCY (Northern Ireland Commissioner for Children and Young People).

United Nations Convention on the Rights of the Child 1989. Available from: www.unhchr.ch/html/menu3/b/k2crc.htm [accessed 31 January 2008]

Wellings, K. et al. (2001) Sexual Behaviour in Britain: Early Heterosexual Experience. *The Lancet*, 358: 9296, 1843–50.

Technical background to the YLT Survey

What is the Young Life and Times Survey?

All too often the opinions of young people are ignored when decisions are made about many of the issues involving them. Thus, the aim of the Young Life and Times (YLT) survey is to record the views of 16-year-olds in Northern Ireland, with a focus on community relations issues such as politics, sectarianism and education. By inviting respondents to suggest topics for the next year's survey, we make sure that the topics covered are relevant to the lives of 16-year-olds in Northern Ireland today.

Links with other surveys

The YLT survey is a sister survey to the Northern Ireland Life and Times (NILT) survey. NILT is an annual survey which has recorded the attitudes and values of adults aged 18 years and over living in Northern Ireland since it began in 1998. The range of topics included in NILT varies each year, although many modules are repeated over time in order to monitor changing attitudes on specific social policy issues. In particular, questions on community relations and political attitudes are included each year in order to track attitudinal change on these issues taking place within the rapidly shifting social and political environment of Northern Ireland. Full details on the NILT survey can be found on the website at www.ark.ac.uk/nilt.

Technical details

Sample

The sample frame for the YLT survey is the Child Benefit Register. Child Benefit is a benefit for people bringing up children and is paid for each child. This is a universal benefit, meaning that it is not means-tested, and every child is eligible. Therefore, the Register contains information on all children for whom Child Benefit is claimed. In 2003, this Register was the responsibility of the Social Security Agency (SSA) of the Department for Social Development (DSD). However, in 2004, while DSD still maintained the database, the responsibility for the payment of Child Benefit transferred to Inland Revenue. Thus, it was necessary to negotiate access to this Register from Inland Revenue, which involved an explanatory memorandum being prepared relating to the Tax Credits (Provision of Information) (Evaluation and Statistical Studies) (Northern Ireland) Regulations 2004.

All young people who celebrated their 16th birthday in February of each survey year are invited to take part. In order to maintain data protection, the survey team does not contact these young people directly. Therefore, all documentation relating to the survey is processed by an independent research organisation.

Advance letter

Fieldwork is undertaken in August – October each year. A letter is posted out to all eligible 16-year-olds, consisting of a letter from DSD, a letter from the project team, a paper questionnaire and a pre-stamped return envelope.

The letter from DSD is addressed to the relevant person and provides an introduction to the survey. It also explains the role of DSD in the project, and confirms that the YLT project team do not have access to names and addresses of the young people in the sample. This letter contains a unique identifier for each person.

The letter from the university project team provides further information about the survey, including the aims of the project, the three possible methods of completing the questionnaire, and details of a prize draw of £500 for which all respondents completing the questionnaire are eligible.

Completing the questionnaire

Respondents are able to choose one of three methods for completing the questionnaire.

1. They can take part by phone, having quoted their identification number.
2. They can complete the questionnaire on-line – quoting their personal identifier to enter that part of the YLT website.
3. They can complete the paper questionnaire that was sent to them in the initial pack and post it back in the pre-stamped envelope.

After one week and after four weeks, reminder postcards and questionnaires are sent out to addressees who had not made contact of any kind.

Survey content

Each year the survey focuses on four or five topics. The range of topics varies every year, although attitudes towards community relations are always covered – see Table 1. Background demographic information is also collected each year.

At the end of each questionnaire, respondents are given the opportunity to identify questions they felt were suitable for inclusion in the following year's survey.

Response rate

Each year, approximately 2,000 questionnaires are sent out. Table 2 shows that the most popular mode of completing the survey was using the paper questionnaire, followed by completing the survey online. Few respondents completed the survey on the phone.

Getting the data

Tables of results from the survey are available on the YLT website within two months of the end of the fieldwork period. For each question, results for males and females and also for the main religious groups can be viewed. Users can download the data in SPSS portable file format from the website to carry out their own statistical analyses. The website also includes the questionnaire in PDF format, as well as technical notes and other publications. The YLT website

Table 1 Survey content

	Year of survey				
	2003	*2004*	*2005*	*2006*	*2007*
Community relations	✓	✓	✓	✓	✓
Cross community contact	✓	✓	✓		✓
Education	✓	✓	✓	✓	✓
Environment and global issues				✓	
Family				✓	✓
Hobbies					✓
Identity	✓	✓	✓	✓	✓
Health (including mental health)		✓	✓	✓	✓
Politics		✓	✓	✓	✓
Poverty					✓
Pressures and influences	✓	✓	✓	✓	✓
Rights					✓
Background	✓	✓	✓	✓	✓

Table 2 Mode of survey completion

	2003	*2004*	*2005*	*2006*	*2007*
Paper	89.2%	97.7%	95.6%	96.0%	95.2%
Online	9.0%	2.2%	4.0%	4.0%	4.8%
Telephone	1.8%	0.1%	0.6%	0%	0%
Total (n)	902	824	819	772	627
Response rate	45.8%	41.6%	40%	39.1%	32.6%

can be found at www.ark.ac.uk/ylt. In addition, a helpline service is available for anyone who has a query about the survey or the results.

Contact information

For all queries relating to YLT, please contact:

Dirk Schubotz, ARK School of Sociology, Social Policy and Social Work, Queen's University Belfast, Belfast BT7 1NN. Tel: (028) 9097 3947. Email: d.schubotz@qub.ac.uk

Index

128

Russell House Publishing Ltd

We publish a wide range of professional, reference and educational books including:

The Child and Family in Context
Developing ecological practice in disadvantaged communities
By Owen Gill and Gordon Jack   2007   ISBN 1-905541-15-7

Working with Black Young People
Edited by Momodou Sallah and Carlton Howson
2007   ISBN 1-905541-14-0

Secret Lives: Growing with Substance
Working with children and young people affected by familial substance misuse
Edited by Fiona Harbin and Michael Murphy
2006   ISBN 1-903855-66-7

For more details on specific books, please visit our website:

www.russellhouse.co.uk

Or we can send you our catalogue if you contact us at:

Russell House Publishing Ltd,
4 St George's House,
Uplyme Road Business Park,
Lyme Regis DT7 3LS,
England.

Tel: 01297 443948.
Fax: 01297 442722.
Email: help@russellhouse.co.uk